# Call Me Uncle Tom?

## Think About It

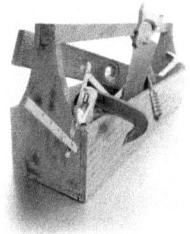

Lillian Thompson

WESTBOW
PRESS®
A DIVISION OF THOMAS NELSON
& ZONDERVAN

WestBow Press books may be ordered through booksellers or by contacting:

WestBow Press
A Division of Thomas Nelson & Zondervan
1663 Liberty Drive
Bloomington, IN 47403
www.westbowpress.com
1 (866) 928-1240

ISBN: 978-1-9736-0439-6 (sc)
ISBN: 978-1-9736-0440-2 (hc)
ISBN: 978-1-9736-0438-9 (e)

Library of Congress Control Number: 2017915711

Print information available on the last page.

WestBow Press rev. date: 08/07/2018

*Memory of Michael 12/29/96-2/15/18*

My son Michael Issac Thompson lived out his legacy of Love strong.
It was so strong that it was his last word on this side.
Jesus left us his spirit of light that continues to carry us through.
Thank You Dad for sharing Michael with us. Your Love continues in the Thompson family.

Lillian D. Thompson

# *Dedication*

First and foremost, I would like to dedicate this book to the author and finisher of it all- Jesus Christ, my Lord and Savior. To the one who led me in the mornings as I woke up to His Word, allowing His truth to go before my story.

To my parents, who were relentless in so many ways in their lives in portraying what was right and wrong, no matter what.

To all of my pastors, present and past, for standing on the Word of God in their daily walks of life.

And with a genuine passion and love I dedicate this to my children, my grandchildren and all of the generations to come. I love you with a forever type of love.

To my husband Morris with much gratitude, honor, and most of all, my love.

Traditionally, *Uncle Tom* would be considered an offensive term in America. Revealing documented truths eliminates traditional thoughts if we choose to take them on.

# Contents

# Acknowledgments

I would like to thank the one who said to me early on that Sunday morning, "Honey, this needs to be heard by others!" Thank you to my patient husband, who was excited and enthusiastic during the extended periods of time of looking at my back and not my face. I love you so much!

I would like to thank my darling daughter Amaris for being my little editor.

I thank all of my children, starting with the oldest Patrice and her loving husband Randy; and my precious grandchildren, Kayla, London, and Jaxon. To my creative Chiara and my theatrical granddaughter, Arianna. Little Morris my oldest son, who I can count on for the complements, and his lovely wife and daughter. Danielle and Scarlett. Miracle Mary, and big hair James Howard, and Michael Issac for their critiques and various views as the book continued to be written. I want you all to know that without your individual lives, this would not be such an interesting story. Thanks for sharing.

Mary Elizabeth, I thank God for your birth, which changed my life. Chiara, thank you for sharing your story. It is a true definition of who you were and are. Love ya.

Thank you, Sadie, for being my constant space invader begging to go outside. Love you too.

Thanks to Sue Reese for telling me to turn it around and tell my story and then editing parts at the beginning of my journey, along with my cheering crowd, her daughters Deanna and Kaylan. You guys are awesome.

To my consistent sister, friend, hang out partner in crime, and prayer buddy, Carole. A big shout out to her family, her ever-so-patient and very soft-spoken husband, Greg, Chervaun and Stephan, and Stephanie and Cherie. Gregory, remember your vision. Kaneshuwa! Gerald I call you a prophet with purpose. Chenelle, keep jumping for the Lord. Thank you all for blessing me with who you are by never changing and always standing strong as a family in the Lord.

Mom Carole, thank you for your giggles. I still want to grow up and be like you.

To my brother in Christ and my nephew through earthly blood, Austin, and his wife, Michele, and Derek and Nathan, Ryan, and Evan, I love you guys. Let's continue to carry the cross.

To my oldest brother, William, and Claudette, thank you for not giving in to my mentality of, "Your grass is greener, so give it up" and helping me to grow.

To my traveling sister, Lola, and her husband, Kenneth, thank you for your stories and encouraging words along the journey of life.

To my brother Michael and his wife Barb, thank you for continuing to stand in your faith in Dutch/Amish country as a family. I thank you, Barb, personally for sharing your family and life experiences that have continued to encourage me as a mom of multiple children to love and cherish.

To my sister, Patricia, and her loving husband, Frank, for overseeing all the care with Mom and Dad, from the housing arrangement to the final resting places. I thank you, Frank, personally for being such a hard worker, which was something Dad admired in you, and so do I.

To my brother-in-law James, continue to walk out your dreams. I will continue to pray that they all come true.

To my sister-in-law Marcella. She and I have a secret love of books, especially the fresh crack of a brand-new book.

To my friend and sister-in-law Edith, I will never forget our special times in Columbus. You will always be my hero and continual overcomer.

To my sister-in-law Liz, who not only bakes the best cookies and brownies but is also one of the best organizers in the world. Keep up the good work, and find your peace spot. Vince, thanks for being the ground for Liz to rest upon, which continues to be stable. It is seen and appreciated.

To my nephew Chuck, first of all, I hope this book explains the silence from me. Man, I've been workin! No, but seriously, Chuck, I love you, and our relationship will always be cohesive. Let us always remember who our Dad is and that we shall never die. We live on forever. I hope you enjoy the book. You are one who can read this book with a great appreciation for where we came from. Thanks for being there for me.

Jeff, what can I say except keep up the good work with your encouraging words of "I feel you "and the classic fist pump and that great smile? To you and your family, Tonya and Little Jeff, let the beat roll on.

To my friend in Cleveland, Lori, thanks for disagreeing with me in love. It did leave a strong impression, more than just a hug and a laugh.

To all of the doctors and nursing staff and all the loving hands involved on that glorious day of birth on the sixth floor at UMMS hospital in Baltimore on July 6, 1992, thank you.

I also would like to thank my loving in-home nursing staff Caroline, Sherie, Mary, Sanora, Caroline, Joann, and Ms. Geraldine, who served from 1993 until 1994. It goes beyond words. I love you all.

A big shout out to Lee Heights Community Church, where the conversations all began from the pulpit to the congregation. Many times it began with my dad with his vibrant amen course, as well as Pastor Vern Miller and Helen Miller and family.

To Village Baptist in Maryland, with Pastor Salmon and his family, thank you for your message on forgiveness.

To Pastor John K. Jenkins and First Lady Trina and family at First Baptist Church of Glen Arden, Maryland. Thank you.

To Pastor and Trina, thank you especially for the day of Mary's birth. Unbeknownst to me, you all jumped in to help us with the children. How you did this is still a mystery. You delivered the message of the birth to our troop. I truly thank our Father for bringing us together for such a time as this. It was and truly is amazing.

Thank you, Pastor David Price and family at Grace Baptist in Maryland for standing on the Word.

Pastor Massenburg, God rest his soul, I thank God for your words of encouragement. First Lady Johnnie, my sister and friend, and family at First Baptist of Midlothian, thank you for giving us our first home church in Virginia.

Pastor Gray and First Lady Jenny at Open Door Baptist, thank you for the in-home Bible studies and the words that continue to resonate: "We shall continue" in the place of abiding .

Thank you to Deacon and Deaconess Little. You all have been a blessing sent from God, especially with the transitions into becoming a grandmother or should I say "Gams," as the girls call me. I thank you for sharing your hearts as we found our lives meshing together in a Father's hands that continue to hold us with security.

Pastor Randy and First Lady Cherie at Faith Landmark in Richmond, Virginia, I thank you for having a home where I truly felt comfortable with my times of breakout praise. We definitely had our times of conversations from the pulpit to the congregation. "Amen!"

And last but definitely not least, to Pastor Mark Becton and First Lady Lori at Grove Avenue Baptist Church in Richmond, Virginia. I thank you, Pastor, for your continual stance on the Word of God as being the truth from the beginning in Genesis to Revelation with much study. I thank you for your encouraging words as I have continued writing. I thank the Lord for using you as a mouthpiece through the process, without you even knowing what was being written. It was as if you had looked over my shoulder on Saturday and decided to give me a personal message on that certain piece. It has been amazing. We shall continue in the Lord as God has called us to be for such a time as this.

To my Demolishing Strongholds class, Hannah, Heath, Megan, Ryan, Justin, Will, Taylor, Emily, Benjamin, and John, thank you for your representations of faith that I have seen in your lives. Continue representing heaven here on earth.

To Christian Youth Theatre of Richmond, Virginia, thanks for being a great family extension. A big shout out to the warehouse, where all the magic happens not only with the sets but with our lives as parents coming out as willing workers wanting all things to be exceptional.

To the Central Virginia Homeschool Athletic Association, for blessing our family on the football field and on the basketball court and on the soccer field—not only for the wins but for the love of Christ. I thank you all for having no shame in your faith and sharing it with our children. Special thanks to Dave and Tracy Hollis for your stamina and your stick-to-itiveness with the football program. I have great appreciation toward your persistence, Tracy, with a heart of a mom in getting a football team started with a few that has grown into many. Go, Disciples!

To Jay and Melanie Horner, thank you for your understanding with the history and standards we continue to train our children up in and as we continue to pray for each other in those realms with a heart of understanding. It only takes a spark to get a fire going. Thanks, Melanie, for the note on my pillow. It sits in the lip of my journal cover whenever I need words of encouragement.

To my real Uncle Tom, who is no longer with us, and Aunt Mable. I would like to thank you for pulling us to the side at the numerous family reunions with that standard you continuously deposited into us.

Edwina, thank you for your shared excitement of history with the family and your diligence in continuing the research and planning with and for the Thompson-Allen family reunion. It is greatly appreciated.

I truly would like to thank my father-in-law and mother-in-law, James and Mary Thompson. I thank you, Dad, for your advice as we continued to come to you in our earlier years of marriage and your continual hand of help. Mom, even though you are no longer with us in body, you still are with us. As I look into Amaris's eyes and watch her mannerisms, there you are. Thank you for sharing. As I watch Patrice with the girls, I remember your words of wisdom toward me as I gently give mine to her. Thank you, and I love you dearly.

I have a heart of thankfulness to a person I never met, but his name shall forever be etched not only on my heart but on my mind: Samuel. I know that your life only lasted a short period of time, but I have chosen to take the time out to not only acknowledge you but to acknowledge your loving mom, Sally, and your dad, Mark, your big brother, Kyle, and your two younger sisters, Mariah and Megan. I thank you, Sally, for sharing Samuel's life with me. It caused me to see life in a whole new light. Thank you!

Without further ado, I would like to stand up and applaud my dad and my mom for raising me to have a different road of life with a detailed trip-tik in hand, the Bible. Thanks, Dad, for sharing your final words on this earth with me so I could share them with others: "I love you."

# Introduction

Who am I? That has been the big question in my life. Many answers came out of traditional thoughts derived from our cultural worldviews that persist in our country today. Some forty-nine years ago, my mother lay across her bed, crying in anger because she was pregnant and she thought it was all my father's fault. That child was me—number five after my parents had recently purchased their first home with four children, the youngest of whom was already thirteen.

I believe that during this period of time, the thoughts that were brewing in my mind were: *Who am I? Why am I here?* With a force of thought as I came down the narrow route of my mother's womb, my mental capacity became crushed by my natural birth. On September 4, 1963, a child was born who was full of curiosity and wonder, coupled with a capacity for fear.

Early in life, I had no real awareness of race other than the foot kind. There was and still is a mental cadence of *ready, set, go!* going on in my life that continues to make me who I am today, with a confidence in knowing my starting mark, my origin.

My quest, you will see, unfolds in the life of a child who then becomes a teenager at risk and an out-of-sync adult, according to the world's ways.

Let's see; I was sexually abused as a child and tried to commit suicide when I was a single, unwed mother still in high school. I became sexually active, which brought on several abortions. However, I was an overcomer who was determined not to be another statistic. At the age of nineteen, I eventually married the man who fathered my first two girls.

After marriage, I went from welfare and the dependent life with a mind-set of, "Since your grass seems more plentiful than mine, it is only right that you should take on the mind-set to help a sister out." If you didn't, I became very offended and a little cynical.

I then found myself being taken by a mind-set that came out of a well-known book called the Bible. I was raised with a faith based on laws that came out of the Bible, which actually drove me away from those words, feeling as though there was no desirable life there. I wanted the good life, and I found it; or should I say, it found me. I was at a point in my life of being sick and tired of being sick and tired.

I found someone who truly loved me. He actually assigned a time in history to send His only beloved Son who lived His life without sinning. Then He took on my sins and died the death that I so deserved. He looked down on me and said in sincerity, "I forgive you, Denise, and I know you know not why you do some of the things you do at times, which actually separates you from the One who truly loves you—our Father who art in heaven."

Who's speaking? Maybe you have heard His name: Jesus. He stood in for me so I could go free. He did it for us all.

Out of the desire I now have, I would like to share my life, like many of our ancestors who were slaves did as they continued to stand, even when with their physical eyes did not see an abundant life. They had an inner knowing of themselves, and they chose to believe and walk it out even unto death at times. This coincides with the title of this book; it was a narrow way, but it did change the minds and hearts of men, not only here in America but all over the world. Let us hate the crime, not the criminal.

Let us listen to the words of Dr. Martin Luther King Jr., who knew his time was drawing to a close. "It may get me crucified,

I may even die. But I want it said even if I die in the struggle that 'He died to make men free.'" I take this opportunity to quote these words, for these are words we normally do not hear quoted by Dr. King, but I take the honor of applying his words here so that those who read them will also have a greater understanding of the man who stood for freedom during the civil rights movement.

Let's look to the one who created us and loves us; trust His Word, not man's. He not only loves me, but He loves us all. I sit here today knowing I am loved, and that is a good feeling to live out until I die mortally, knowing I will take on my new form of life and live forever in the ways of love. Now let's get up and accept these words to be true and live our lives in abundance. Love is not just for now but forever and ever.

"Who am I? Why am I here?" I found myself taking on a truth that I believe as a standard that has not shifted or changed. Before I was in my mother's womb, I was in the hands of God. I am a creation of God's thoughts put into order and held together by His Word. I am in this world with many ideas. However, there are many ways of living out our truths, whatever we tend to hold on to and live out as a truth. I hold on to a kingdom of God, mentality taking dominion and holding a position of adoption, of a princess. It is all mine, and I am response-able. My responses are dictated by the Word of God, which is my constitution in this world while not being *of* this world.

Chapter 1

# Foundations of My Faith

*Growing up in Cleveland, Ohio,* in the late sixties and going to a Mennonite church, my thoughts of truth were taught to me at church, home, and of course, at school. The Mennonite faith was law based from the Old Covenant as opposed to the grace found in the New Covenant, although they believed in Jesus Christ. I felt a responsibility to believe from the home that what my parents were living out in their religious beliefs was true, as it was being demonstrated before me daily. As I walked past their cracked bedroom door and saw my father on his knees praying about current-day issues—mainly my issues—it made me wonder who or what his faith was in. In the bathroom on a portable floor cabinet sat the Daily Bread, without a doubt on that day's date; these were my mother's daily readings. In the car, Christian music played constantly, if the Cleveland Indians weren't playing.

In preparation for the Bible studies that took place in our home, the aroma of freshly brewed coffee awaited the church guests. My parents were nowhere near perfect, but what their lives displayed before me was a constant leaning on the Word as manifested in the Bible, a truth to live out.

My father was the elder emeritus of the church. His responsibilities were to pray for the church families and be an overseer in the congregation. He was close friends with the pastor, who, by the way, was Caucasian. As I take these thoughts captive, I realize why at times it was difficult for me to see racial differences as a youth. After a bike accident, I had received a pretty bad head concussion. My parents were not comfortable leaving me with just anyone during this time, but I remember being able to stay at the pastor's house. They had five children, and we were all just one big, happy family. There was a trust that I recognized and thought was the norm.

My mother was a housewife by trade. Her second job was cleaning the church, and my dad and I would go to help. It was routine, just a part of our daily lives. She only worked outside of the house after I was in high school, when she went to clean a woman's house. That continued for a couple of years. She also would iron workmen's dress shirts for a dollar a shirt. My mom was always home when I returned from school; I felt a great security in that, and while walking home, no matter what the situations were at school that day, I knew I was coming home to someone who loved me.

I am the youngest of five children, with my closest sibling thirteen years older than myself. My parents were married for approximately sixty-seven or sixty-eight years before my father passed away at the age of ninety-two in 2007. He left a legacy of five children, all married with children and grandchildren and great-grandchildren. On the day of his funeral, there I sat with my husband of twenty-four years and our seven children, two grandchildren, and last but not least, our son-in-law. I looked around on that day. I saw a garden with a variety of flowers containing seeds of faith that had been lived out by my parents, not only within our immediate family but also with the church.

Our family was very active in the church, from Sunday school teachers to choir directors to youth group leaders. My brother went off to Honduras on a mission trip. My sister went to Central Christian High School, where she stayed with another Caucasian family. One of my brothers and sisters went to Goshen Christian College in Goshen, Indiana. All of these arenas of life were being played out before a little girl who did not recognize race but a sense of family. There was no real acknowledgment of race or separation due to race that I can recall.

Then the school I attended purposed to teach me a new and different truth—the world's truth. I felt a little out of place at times because my school was in an African American neighborhood. I started to feel like I had to be a little different to be accepted in this group. I could dance with some moves here and there. When it came to having a tough side, the best card I could play stemmed from my older sister's children, my age and older, who lived in the village. When you knew someone who lived in the village, more than likely they could fight or at least knew someone who could. I started to see a difference not in race but in what we as a people group recognized and viewed as a truth. There was a difference as to where you lived and whether you were light skinned or dark skinned among the African Americans, if you had good hair that didn't require relaxers versus tightly curled hair that required chemicals. There was a stigma among this general people group that straight hair was better. There was a higher recognition of race when you claimed that you were Indian, not Black.

I started to learn a different view of truth in the public school that made me very inquisitive at home and at church. The confusion set in even more when my parents sent me to Lumen Cordium, a Catholic high school. I said my Hail Marys as I went to confession for my sins. Being surrounded with a view of racial difference and finding myself in the minority, not only racially but within the realm of religious customs, I found myself in the realm of, "Good is what you make it, no matter where you stand." I became the good girl at church and the bad girl on the streets. It all depended on the surroundings and what was needed for the moment, be it good or bad. I was good at playing the parts.

In school I learned about millions of years of death and destruction and dinosaurs. Being displayed before me in museums, artwork, and science books was information that pointed to monkeys turning into humans. I had evidence right before my eyes, and my parents didn't even oppose this new perspective. When I started to compare and ask questions concerning the Bible stories and my studies in science at school, many sessions ensued at the kitchen table, where my parents were not able to back up the stories to defend the Bible against what I was learning in school. All they would tell me was to just believe. At that point, my family's faith began to wane for me, and I invented my own faith that became more real to me day by day. My identity was whatever I made it out to be until things went wrong and I needed a truth with hope backing it up.

As I grew up, I found myself in various situations that made me question what love was. I had been sexually abused as a child several times over, mainly by a neighbor's son. There was a time when I was on a cross-country trip with my parents and their close friends. At one of our sleepovers, my parents and their friends took the opportunity to go out for the night. While they were gone, the young man who they had left me with took advantage of me. It all started with him touching my hair and telling me how pretty I was. This was always an alarm for me, and I screamed out in my mind, "It is all about to happen again!" The pain, secret winks, and gentle pats made me feel like I was marked for life. I was confused and really did not want to know what love was all about if it involved things like this. My thoughts were totally out of sorts, and I felt lost and stripped of myself.

I wondered if it would be possible to know true love. Then I met Morris.

Chapter 2

# Looking for Love

W*hen I met Morris, it* was during baseball season. Our church had a softball team that was actually pretty good. One day during practice, this guy who was invited out to play with our team was welcomed by just about everyone except for me. I thought he was arrogant and just plain cocky. I was practicing on the pitcher's mound, so there was a moment of small talk, which I really could do without while he was at bat. I found out that he was a pretty good player, so his presence was good for the team.

During one of our tough games, we were down by two runs. Morris came to me and asked if I could go to the movies with him. My answer was, "Sure, if we win this game." Mind you, we were in the bottom of the ninth inning, with two runners on base and two outs, and Morris was up to bat. Well, when he hit that home run, I made a run for my sister's green mustang and told her, "Let's go, now!" He did finally catch up with me, and I found out that he actually wasn't one of the bad guys.

At least from my eyes, at that time in my life I was yearning for someone who could rescue me from all the pain I was carrying within. Morris was the one who was willing to listen, and at times it still is his strong physical hold that continues to make me feel secure. He is the type of person who speaks out without fear with an understanding that continues to make others alert and ready to respond around him as to why they think or feel the way they do with clear explanation. These attributes can sometimes come off as if he is arrogant or cocky. However, he is a standup guy for what he believes in, and he will speak out without fear. Seeing this rare character trait in an individual appealed to me, which brought on a great curiosity to know more about this young man. I found out through conversations with others that Morris was one of the basketball stars on the Shaker Heights High School basketball team, which wasn't the winning ticket for me.

As you will decipher from the occurrences of my life as they unfold, Morris and I were not just talkers; we found ourselves closer than we had planned, with situations that turned out to be blessings in our lives. As teenagers, we had great challenges to overcome because of the choices we made. There was teen pregnancy, or should I say I became a young mother.

I was not willing to be marked as a failure or take it on like the crowd that surrounded me that had their ideas of what the norm was in these common situations. There was something different about me. I had a passion, drive, and surge burning from within that I acknowledged, and it took me on roads of the uncommon in life, which turned out better than I could ever imagine. One thing that I can say did get better was my search for love. I can say that what I have found so far has and continues to get better than I could ever imagine.

## Attitude Adjustment

Morris and I planned not just our wedding but discovered where we would start our lives together as a family. We started out early, with our oldest daughter being three years old and with one on the way. All of these items being in place at this time affected our thinking toward where we would live economically. As we searched on the east side of Cleveland, we could not find an area that we felt would give us sufficient comfort in raising our family.

While we lived in Cleveland, there were some things I noticed as I started to live outside of my father's and mother's way of living. There were very strong boundaries of race and culture from a traditional understanding of who we all were and our places and right positions to live and grow as individuals in certain areas. It was all okay as long as you knew your place.

I realized this after we were married when we decided to live on the west side of town. The initial repercussions that came out of it were not all productive. For example, when we moved into our third-floor apartment, we were welcomed that evening with a brick being thrown through our daughter's bedroom window. I just thank the Lord that she was not in bed when this occurred and no one was hurt.

It did cause us to be even more on our guard than usual. When I took on an attitude of there being a difference, I began to take on a different approach with others according to the color of our skin, which was a rare thing for me.

## What Are the Best Schools in the Area?

There was one positive impression from our experiences living on the west side that I want to share with you, a precursor of things to come. It was a nontraditional way of teaching that made me stop and think.

My husband was still finishing out his last year of college, and he was holding at least two jobs at this time. I had been working also until we had to downsize to one working outside the home while I became the more traditional homemaker, as my mother had been.

My husband developed a relationship with his boss, who invited us out to his home one day. He had expressed his faith to my husband, which was not the invitation that brought our family to his home; it was a job opportunity with accounting and the possibilities of a move to San Antonio that grabbed our attention.

While we were visiting, I noticed a peace in their home that was quite rare—so rare that it drew my attention. It seemed like they were in a different race. They weren't trying to prove to me that they were swamped with business, be it family or office. It was, to be honest, kind of weird.

During our conversations, we started to talk about schools. Now brace yourself; this was in 1983, and what they told me was so out of the water that it kept me on the question button, which I'm sure for them was a bit amusing, as I think back on the situation for myself. They were a part of that taboo world known as homeschoolers. That was the topic of our conversation for a while.

## A Part of Society

We did eventually move from the west side of town but not to San Antonio. We moved back to the east side in the area my husband grew up in called Shaker Heights. We were very excited about this move because it put us in the right position, or so we thought. The schools had a great reputation, as they still do today as far as I know. Even though everything looked to be in the right order, it was all like a cover up; the mask of, "I'm okay and so are you," was being painted on my face ever so lightly.

As time moved on, I felt like I was shedding layers of an underclassman trying my hardest not to flunk out of the university of life. There were the cheaters in life who had ideas they would share with me that they felt were the cliff notes of life, such as welfare and drugs, the sedatives that made it all feel good, or so I thought. It was a way of having a similarity to life but not the full deal, just bits and pieces. I had stopped going to church every Sunday and attending Bible study and all of those customary ways of life because it did not appeal to me any longer.

Diligently we pursued integrating ourselves into the community, understanding that the impressions we made were also impressions of our family, especially my husband's, since they lived in the city at this time. His family had a very high standing in the area, and it became a bit of a tight squeeze. I felt the pressure of the expectations on me as a mother and a wife but most importantly as an outstanding citizen in the area. It was the underlying issue of the questions, "When are you going to start your career in the higher echelon of society?" Motherhood was smiled upon, but the bigger deal was the career, which I gave up on to take care of the babies. There was also the secret society of, "You can't commit to the marriage, you must commit to the career; it won't let you down, but remember, the man will. Always ready yourself for the fall of man."

## The Train Stops Here!

After having a miscarriage and almost losing our second daughter due to gamma seizures, our time in Shaker Heights was slowly but surely coming to a close. Our final days spent in the city were spent right across the street from where my husband was raised as a child. It was a very interesting time. I got to know my second set of parents quite well on a day-to-day basis. Let's just say we were very neighborly, to say the least. I call my father-in-law Dad. It is a very endearing term for me because he was and still is a great dad.

I remember the days of our parents sitting on the front porch after a delectable meal that only my mother-in-law could produce. You might have to wait awhile, but it was all worth it. There were always special arrangements added to surround the meal with elegance at all times.

My mother-in-law is no longer with us, but I am so thankful for all she shared with me, not only with understanding me as her daughter-in-law, but as a mother, to bring clarity to the strains of motherhood. I remember her saying to me within a year of her passing that she didn't know how I did it but she was proud of the way things were working out. She admired my faith concerning my children and her grandchildren. She also shared with me a great appreciation for my faith, which I will never forget. Thank you, Mom.

As we continued to peruse that great city of Cleveland, we found our final destination in a city called Warrensville Heights. We lived in a townhouse, which was an actual downsize from the house we lived in when we lived across the street from my in-laws.

I was holding a job as an early childhood educator at a daycare center. I was expecting our third child, and we were really excited when we found out he was a boy.

I remember the day my father-in-law took me to the hospital for the ultrasound. When I came out and told him it was a boy, you would have thought a spotlight had been turned on. His face just beamed with such pride. This was news of his first grandson, and Dad became the news bearer.

My husband and I had planned to have only three children because it was getting out of hand, and the train had to stop here in order for us to have any life, or so we thought.

**Learning to Embrace Peace**

While we were living in Warrensville, my nephew—my oldest sister's son, from the village—and I became very close. One day, of course, out of the blue early in the morning my husband got a call from the hospital. It was my nephew. There was a tragic accident where he was hit by a car while working downtown. This incident caused sudden random feelings, such as anger, passion, fear, and confusion from several family members and friends.

It's something how tragedy can draw some of us out while for others it will create a final exit in our thinking through our emotions, determining where we are standing in life when those sudden occasions occur.

Since my nephew was disabled to the extent that he could not walk and was in need of extensive care when he was discharged from the hospital, he ended up with his father who lived a few doors down from us in our townhouse.

This is where we found ourselves when the day before the phone call we were looking at houses in the surrounding areas. We were feeling a bit out of sync with the family and the societal overall traditional borders that existed in the area. The veil was being lifted through our house hunting. The selections that were being offered to us were causing frustration. My husband and I were feeling like it wasn't time to move, and we decided to stop looking at that time. These situations with the house hunting and my nephew caused us to stop and capture some sort of produced thought as to the next step in life. We needed to make decisions with purposeful direction. My purposeful direction of thought became zoned in an area of a need with my nephew's rehabilitation, which I was in position to fill willingly with love.

As we continued to all grow physically and mentally healthier, our lives started to become less bound. I found myself one day sitting with a good friend of mine who was my nephew's girlfriend, discussing something surrounding my nephew's condition. With tensions being so great, our conversation turned into a heated debate. We found ourselves in tears, saying to each other that it was okay for us to agree to disagree and still be friends. We actually ended up laughing and embracing each other with a precious moment of peace.

At this point in time, the majority of my confrontations started with an awareness of myself before the Word of God. It boiled down to this: either you agree or you don't but it is what it is. I decided to stand on a truth, and it was Jesus from the cross saying to me, "I forgave you. Now it's time for you to forgive others when they know not what they do as they choose to turn away from Me, as you have also chosen to turn away from Me." I made a decision to make a turn around and believe His Word.

## Are We Moving from Cleveland?

My husband had started to do more traveling, which left me with more confrontations since my stand-up man who did not take any stuff was not there. We were feeling a little trapped in the Cleveland mode of life. We were growing tired of the stagnant ways of thinking at that time, and we had a strong desire to get out as soon as possible.

My husband found himself in Washington, DC, for a business conference, and while he was there networking, he found himself talking with an individual who offered him a job in DC and asked if he would send his resume. The company would set him up with an interview, and they also invited the family to come. When he called me with the news, it was all I could do to hold back my somersaults of, "Yipee! We are finally getting out of here!"

He came home with such excitement that there was a small party dance held in our house that night. We were so ready to go that we could just taste new beginnings in our lives as a family. The final moment of excitement came with a phone call from Washington, DC, which basically sounded to me like,

"Pack your bags, Thompson family of five. This train is here for you! All aboard!" We are leaving Cleveland as a family to start anew and become that uncommon family that we felt a burning desire to be.

## Someone's Moving

While this was our first experience of a big move I, believe it was also a first time of a big move in our townhouse complex. The Allied truck pulled up, and there was barely enough room for it to sit in the parking lot. It was a spectacle; neighbors unknown were out walking past our unit. I will remind you now this was not normally a walkabout neighborhood, but it was to the extreme on the two days of our moving.

A little girl pressed her face up against our screened door and asked, "What are ya'll doing in there?"

Mind you now as you cast your judgments on my actions, I was a natural baby in Christ, excited about an escape, or so I believed. I told her, "Non'ya!"

With a confused look on her face, she said, "What did you say?"

Then I repeated it and said, "None of your business." Not to justify my actions, but the little girl was known to be a bit irritating and extremely nosey.

We said our final good-byes to friends and family, taking lots of pictures, giving hugs and kisses, saying many prayers, and greeting well-wishers. There was also the negative of, "Are you sure? This may not be the best move." We often heard the phrase, "You don't have as much family down there!" There was a looming feeling of sharks being in the water, so we had to be careful as we jumped.

We respected our parents' words and honored them in our decision making at the final signings for my husband's new position in Washington, DC. I will never forget how dogmatic my father-in-law was on the insurance. At times for me it was a little irritating, but I will say here, honor those words of wisdom because there will be a day when they will pay huge dividends in the end.

As we drove away, what continued to roll through my mind was, *Forgive them, for they know not what they do. Amen*

Chapter 3

# New Beginnings

I*t was so refreshing to* look for a home in a new area. It freeing not only mentally but geographically—until we realized the increase in pay was not as great as it would have been in Cleveland. The life that surrounded us in Maryland made it seem all the better. We found a quaint townhouse in Bowie unlike the one in Warrensville. It was an actual house with three levels of living space. We were excited and ready to live our lives away from Cleveland.

Our initial gravitational pull of relationships was with my oldest brother and his wife and family who had lived in the area for I believe almost twenty years at that time. Since they were acquainted with the area, we gave in to their discernments quite heavily. They live in Mitchellville, and in 1988, they directed us to search in Bowie, which was a beautiful rural part of Maryland. They called it at that time living in the sticks.

As we began our lives in Maryland, we would hang out with them quite a bit until there was a day of a rude awakening for me that caused me to grow up and trust my own footing with the decisions I made with my family. On that day, a storm went through and our electricity went out. I called my brother's house with an old-school way of thinking that when everything is not working properly, you should rely on your relatives. Well, my sister-in-law, who is one of the sweetest people in this world, delivered a hard message, and she did it with kindness. What she expressed was that we must rely on our own resources. She started to explain to me how she and my brother would make it through tough times when they only had each other to rely on. It was a hard pill to swallow, but she was right. It was a day of trusting in what I had instead of looking over the fence with an assumption that there are things that you have that could supply my needs. It was a well-prescribed pill that I needed to take to survive at this time.

Moving during the summer months was good timing for the plans we had for starting the girls in a new school. A lack of knowledge of the school and the school's systems gave me great concerns. My nerves were pretty frayed, with our oldest daughter who was currently in the third grade and her sister who was starting kindergarten. I found out quickly that all of my children carry strong differences. Our oldest had a hard time separating from me when she started school in Cleveland so I was bracing myself for the worst with the younger daughter. However, I found out quickly that there was a different tune on the first day of school. It went like this: "Mom, let me catch the bus, please." I released her, and she did well. Actually, they both did very well in adjusting to the new school.

## Separation

The family separation did take its toll. One late night after the house had settled into its quiet mode, we were startled from our rest by a loud knock at the front door. My husband rushed down the stairs to open the door, and there was a police officer with flashlight in hand talking to my husband. I could not understand what was being said. I believe that the pulse of my heart was overtaking my ability to hear. As I was standing at the top of the stairs, a little person came out from between them and plodded up the stairs, head down, covered in a red hood. I went to turn on the hallway light, not expecting to see any of our children, for they were all in bed. No! I was missing one, and there she stood, our oldest daughter, who was running away to go back to Cleveland to be with her grandma.

Obviously this took me into a pattern of making things right or making them look right. The first attempt was through the counselor at the new school and of course talking with my mom. She, by habit I felt, would say, "We will pray about it. God knows what is best."

My response was a bland, "Thanks, Mom."

Then she would follow that up by saying, "Have you all found a church yet?"

The answer once again was, "Not yet, Mom."

**Get Active**

My mindset now was set in a busyness of activities to make all things right in the eyes of men. The guilt of condemnation played strong on the cords of my life. A way of living life according to what felt right at the time—"Just do it!"—was leading my mindset, with no strong boundaries. I was a big girl; I could choose what is right and what was wrong and make it work.

As far as the children, we needed to get them involved in various activities of interest, such as sports, dance, church, etc. We did get involved with a church that was right around the corner, close enough if we wanted to walk, we could. I went to a community center, which provided a list of many age-appropriate activities. We got our oldest daughter and her sister signed up with basketball. I enrolled our baby boy in a class called rumble tumble for toddlers. Our Saturdays were now recognized as game days, to be scheduled out and acknowledged very strongly, especially by my husband. With him being the coach or at least assistant coach, these days became almost like our Sundays for me growing up. This worked out well for a while.

When we first started to attend the church, we received a call from the pastor to set up a house visit. Well, when the pastor's day of visitation came, I went into our refrigerator and took all the wine coolers and placed them behind the milk. I just wanted to be able to open the refrigerator without guilt. Having the rattling bottles of coolers in the door just would not look right.

Our children came out and greeted the pastor appropriately. My husband was able to talk about work and his responsibilities in the community as a coach and the families we had met in this arena. I chimed in with background info about our religious background with my family in Cleveland, which matched up with a lot of the customs of the church family. I came out of this meeting feeling pretty good about this perfect picture I was painting, or so I thought.

I fell right into the religious pattern quite easily. I joined the choir, of course. That to me is the first step of engrafting yourself into the congregation. All the children went to Sunday school. My husband was not comfortable with going to Sunday school, so I became a Sunday school teacher. It all worked.

My activities changed I registered as a student at the community college to finish up with my credits to acquire my teaching degree. I was attending two days a week. My classes started early in the day after the girls went off to school. It was really cool. As I was driving to class, there was a radio station I found myself frequently listening to, and on these mornings they would play the same song. At the end of the song, they would have someone recite the Lord's Prayer, which was a very familiar prayer for me as a child. We weren't that heavy into praying at this time unless there was something wrong, and it was a holding hands moment of public or private prayer. Every time the prayer would come on, I would pray with them, it was a time I constantly looked forward to.

## Visitations

As our family and friends began to visit us, it was so exciting. We were able to accommodate pretty much anyone's kind of lifestyle. If you were into partying, we were the people to visit who had class. For the churchgoers, we had a church we were affiliated with and had the "God is good" crowd of individuals when needed.

Our parents were very proud of us. My in-laws were familiar with the area as they told us of their times in the past of courting and having children and the excitement of the move altogether. Mom Thompson had attended Bowie State. As lieutenant colonel in the army, Dad took us over to Fort Meade to shop one time at the commissary. That was fun and enriching. We really enjoyed our times down on the mall in DC at the monuments hearing their tales of good times in life.

I will never forget one day we went to the Smithsonian Museum with Mom and Dad Thompson, and they started reminiscing as we were listening to music selections that they knew quite well. Dad gestured to Mom and said, "You know back in the day, your mother and I used to cut a rug!" Mom countered with, "What do you mean used to!" Then she began to do the Jitterbug, and the kids joined in. These are great times to be remembered.

Our friends came down, and we were able to show them the town. My niece would come over and watch the kids, and we would take on the night life. Of course we went to the more classy clubs of drinking and socializing.

My nephew who had the accident came down with his girlfriend. For a time, our house had a feeling of Grand Central

Station, and we were loving all of the attention and the love being poured out on both sides.

After the visits tapered down and life became more set in, I started to get to know my close neighbors and my sisters and brothers from church. We became closer to them, and instead of the "God is good" crowd, we found ourselves in a more family atmosphere. After the in-home women's Bible study groups and the affiliations going past VBS, our extensions in relations became closer. The girls started in ballet class, which of course is one of the things one of my sisters at church did for a living out of her home. She had a beautiful home set in the country with an extension on the home that was the studio for dance classes.

## The Trail of Forgiveness

While we attended Village Baptist Church, the Lord touched my heart with His Word on forgiveness, which caused me to think back on my days of exit from Cleveland, and He took it to another level. I became convicted, and the words that followed were not my own. I found myself forgiving a predator who had preyed on me as a young child. I had buried it deep within the recesses of my mind. It was that long-lost tell-tale heart still pulsating with the face of the neighbor's oldest son as he would take his liberties to sexually assault or in better terms rape me at the tender age of three or four. My forgiveness toward him was awkward to say the least. It was not face to face or with a phone call; it was from within. I truly forgave him, and all of a sudden there was a lightness within me, as if I were free from a heaviness that resided within my soul. I found myself calling some of my relatives without wanting a response. I just had a willingness for them to hopefully receive my changed heart. There really are things we do that we do not know are causing us to be distant—not only to one another but to the one who created us and loves us.

Chapter 4

# The School of Confrontation

As times continued and our finances seemed to be a little tight, I decided to start a daycare center out of my home. I had to put a hold on school, but I still strongly desired to become a teacher one day.

From previous experiences of my daycare days in Cleveland, I took what I had learned in that teaching atmosphere and downsized it to fit my home. I took in three children and a couple of afterschool children from the neighborhood. It was a blessing to have the children and teach them, especially the naptimes. I was a fan of the neighborhood library. Actually, I still am; some things never die.

I started extending myself with my clients, and it became a little stressful. When I had things to do with my children, my time was not respected, and for some of the parents it was more of an afterthought. It became an issue I had to confront. I was not characteristically strong at this, but it had to be done.

I found that confrontation does not mean you are a bad or arrogant person. It did give me a changed perspective that if I truly cared about a situation, I would not stand back and wait for someone else to say something out of sympathy for my situation.

Standing up and confronting a situation causes a notice of

attention not just from one party but from both individuals, and the two can then look at the issue and come up with some type of resolution. This is what occurred in my home. We all chose our different directions in life accordingly, with peace being the orchestrator of the whole.

## What to Judge

I did find myself a little quick to cast judgment on others after that situation, as though now everybody only saw me as the woman who was very kind and would watch your children. A new neighbor moved in, and they had two children. She came to my steps after the school bus took off. I had to let her know that I was not taking on any more children in my home, if that was the reason she had come my way. I stood there unsure but knowing that this was not going to happen again.

She says even to this day that I was about to bite her head off, but I really do not believe I was that brash. She later became one of my dearest friends. We became walking buddies; she also introduced me to thrift store shopping, which I really got a kick out of. It led me into finding treasures in the least-expected places. She gave me the inspiration to enjoy being a homemaker. She is a seamstress, and at the time she was working from her home.

Walking the neighborhood and talking about God was how our relationship started. She attended a Catholic church, while my church was Baptist. We didn't look at each other as denominations; we looked at each other as two women wanting to know more about the one who we both believed in and loved us. Everything we did we enjoyed, and we truly gave God credit for it from our hearts. It was and is pretty cool.

I will never forget on one of our initial days of walking, we decided that before we would go out and walk, we would read some passages out of the Word of God, and then we would walk for about forty minutes and talk about what that meant to each of us specifically. That was our Magic Kingdom. Sometimes we would agree and other times not so much, but it was all good. One day on our walk we went walking by our two churches. Her church doors were open, and she asked me to come in with her and pray, and I did. That was pretty cool. After we finished praying together, we proceeded with our walk. That has been our relationship, and to this day it continues. It's something to think about that is awesome.

## Home, Health, Care

One day I get a call from Cleveland concerning my sister who is closest in age to me. She was diagnosed with breast cancer. It struck me dumb. This was the sister of zeal, so hearing this just threw me for a loop. Not long after this report, my sister who was living in Jamaica came back to the States for similar circumstances. Since she worked for the government, she had to return to DC. My older sister's test also came out malignant, positive for breast cancer.

At this time, my older sister wanted to go to a church that I believe she had visited already. At that time we were in search of peace and a grasp on some type of understanding. For my sister and me both, we found it in the church.

This church, unlike the church right down the street, was a little different. It was a Baptist church, but it was situated in a different area. Let's just say the congregation and the pastor looked more like me! It was, should I say, a little more up tempo and I could get into the praise and worship.

In our church in Cleveland, my father was one of the few people who every now and then would respond to what the pastor was saying, and at this church there was a pulpit-to-congregation conversation that I could agree with and join in with excitement.

After I attended this church with my sister, I invited my husband to come out. I felt that since his family had attended a church in Cleveland that had a similar flair, he might be more willing to go to this specific church. At the church we had been attending as a family, it started to be more of me and less of us as a family.

My husband not only liked the new church, but he went forward and joined the church, which was a little out of order for me since I already had a church home. As a matter of fact, as the pastor came to greet us so warmly into the congregation, I kindly retorted with, "Not so much with me. I already have a church home. I will pray about it." He responded with a smile of agreement.

I was a little confused about what to do in this situation since I was in the choir and had teaching commitments that tied me with our community church. I tried to attend both churches for a little while until I was hard pressed to make a decision.

At the church my husband was attending, I felt more peace because we went as a family. The Lord tugged at my heart with that submission thing, which was a difficult pill to swallow, but I took it and it wasn't too bad. It actually turned out good. I found myself with mind-changing experiences with a different realm of good and what it truly means. I was starting to trust in this Word of God for myself, and I was starting to feel a little weird.

Both of my sisters recovered. While I was going through these deep wounds, it drew me into a prayer relationship that I remembered having as a child, and it saved me. Instead of constantly breaking down and calling on others, I began to rely on what I already had, and it was with a simple faith revelation. The readings with my walking buddy continued. Actually, they became even more spiritual.

**I've Got a New Attitude**

At this point in time in my daily life, I had started working at Sears in their catalog department. It was exciting, starting in one position on the register and then finding myself being promoted to different positions. My final position was in a department called home improvements, which consisted of a more office atmosphere where I scheduled out department representatives. The job came with labels and "Ring the bell, your scores are the highest today." It became a more stagnant time of my life when I felt like I was becoming more complacent, but all the while there was a bigger picture of life that I knew not of, even though each step was with purpose.

We found a neighborhood doctor who was really kind and conscientious with all of his patients. Sometimes I would notice the patients in the waiting room becoming a little anxious, and I could understand their frustrations. The doctor would talk with all of his patients with sincerity, which meant time was elapsing. I saw an opportunity to improve his business by eliminating his need to escort his patients in and out of the examination rooms. As this continued, I could tell that this doctor and his wife, who was running the front desk, were a bit overwhelmed. I commented on it and said in jest, "If I could, I would be willing to help you guys." In turn he offered me a job.

I came in for an interview, and we were all so excited I was excited for them because I could see the good and I did not want it to end. I was willing to help in any way I could. I was their assistant, and it was a wonderful change in my life. Not only was I helping the doctor and his wife, but I was also able to talk with people and encourage them. I came to find out that I was made to build up others, and I thrived because of it. There was a definite leading from within back then and even more so now as I acknowledge it.

All was well for some time as I continued to work as the assistant to the doctor. He was considered at that time to be a general physician. The patients ranged from newborns getting their first outing to be checked by the doctor to those seasoned ones who were looking for someone to talk to about their hurts and pains physically and mentally. The office clientele began to increase by leaps and bounds. I remember one of the things I became very proficient in was starting up the new patient file and ensuring that all the appropriate questions were asked so there would be no glitches for the patient and definitely not for the doctor.

The hours were increasing, and my time was starting to be consumed in the office. They were very lenient toward me having the children in the office with me, especially our son, who was only four years old at the time. I would bring in puzzles and coloring books and various quiet playtime activities for him, without forgetting the occasional snack for a growing little boy. I started to feel a little bit out of order when my ten-year-old daughter, who was now a latch-key child, called the office to tell me that her seven-year-old sister had run away.

While all of these things were taking place, the doctor and his wife had leased us their house. Things were happening so fast, but it was all good. I just felt as though I was trying to catch up with the ride assigned for me on the merry-go-round of life. As far as our daughter, all things were fine, but deep down inside I was thinking, *Is everything okay or am I missing something?* I had lost an extreme amount of weight. My persona had changed from homemaker to the businesswoman of the day. Our finances were good. We were well on our way to being first-time home buyers. All was well, or so I thought. My sites were now changing, to nursing of course, as I saw myself as the future LPN of the office.

My extreme weight loss happened because my walking buddy and I were becoming the well-known walkers of the neighborhood. Not only were we walking, we were also doing some aerobics with some light weight training involved. Our church attendance was increasing, or should I say my husband was becoming closer to the pastor, and we were becoming closer with their family as well.

## Deja vu

One day my older sister, who was now living in the area and also attending the same church, called me and asked if I would be interested in going over to the pastor's house to help them out by cleaning their house. Well of course I went. In our family, we would not only do anything for our pastor but for those in need.

One time when I was younger in Cleveland, my family, including my sister and her family did some work together. My sister's oldest son is two years older than I am, her second son is one year older than I am, and her youngest daughter is two years younger. Needless to say, we are close in age. Well, we all came together to clean up an abandoned house for a family. I never knew the family. All I knew was that it was to help someone out, and everyone was very diligent with their individual chores. Cleaning up someone's house who was in need was a no brainer for me.

While cleaning up their house, I became convicted not because of something that was said but because of the way I was feeling about what I was viewing. The church's first lady was like the friend I never had met until now, and their children were just regular children, reminding me of my own. As I looked around their house while cleaning I noticed numerous teaching posters with numbers and objects, an alphabet train, and words on various objects around the house. I said, "Hey!

What's going on here?" I was feeling that same feeling I felt when we met that family in Cleveland. I asked the big question, "Do you teach your children from home?" And she responded with a joyful "Oh, yes!" Wow, this really threw me for a loop. This was not the only one that I would find myself jumping through as life continued.

Our relationship with the pastor and his wife continued to grow. She would continuously question me on the subject of homeschooling. I had shared with her, on that day that we were at their home, about how I thought it was so weird that I felt something drawing me into homeschooling.

Now she was able to answer a lot of those lingering questions, like, "How?" and "Why does this make sense?" She would laugh and say, "I really think the Lord is calling you to homeschool," and I would answer with, "Not me, girlfriend." My conviction was that I was going to school to be a teacher. I loved helping others, and here I was not willing to not only teach my children but to take care of them with attentions I was pouring out almost daily, with excitement, for others.

### Isn't the Quiver Full?

My relationship with the doctor and his wife was also growing. We had actually had dinner at their house. We were like one big happy family. His wife and I would share recipes, especially her delicious Indian cuisine. I still have some of those recipes. The chapatti was delicious.

We would talk to each other with a sense of love toward each other as we all consumed ourselves with the office activities. One day, while noticing the increase in business, the doctor mentioned to me that he would need to hire another individual in the office, which I agreed to wholeheartedly. At the same time, his wife was talking about pulling out, which I believed was a good move because they had one child at home, even though the grandparents were watching her. I strongly believed that it was a good idea for her to go home.

While deep down inside I am genuinely excited for them, at the same time I was feeling the pangs in my heart about my position as a mother and wife. What was keeping me focused was the money, and the status that I believed I was earning.

With our three beautiful children—two girls and one boy—our family was perfect! My motto was, "Three is enough for me," until a change took place in our lives that required some radical faith.

It was when my husband was attending a financial freedom seminar at the church. He was also on the financial committee, which caused my husband to have double duty, so he asked if I would sit in on this session and take notes. Well, of course, no problem!

Well, not until the speaker started addressing the issue of children being a blessing from God. I struggled with his message, including a scenario of his family at the dining room table, having chairs empty that could have been filled if they were not in the position of blocking the Lord's blessings. I was thinking, *Where in the world is he going with this?* Then it hit me when he opened up about his wife having her tubes tied. I was thinking, *What is so bad with that?* There I sat with my tubes tied, and "Three is enough for me." End of story.

Not really. My husband was lingering around and heard the presenter's testimony. He came over to me with that look that made me quiver inside. He has these big eyes that speak louder than words, and that was how the three began in the first place. He proceeded to put his hand on my leg and just ever so gently squeezed. *Now what?* I was thinking to myself. After the class ended, he said to me, "I think the Lord is speaking to us." My immediate response was, "I don't think so!"

## I Have to Quit My Job!

Let us stop here for a selah moment, which means a moment to think on this one, if you don't mind.

Hopefully you got the picture. It was a walk by faith and not by sight. There were no special-interest groups to sign up for with this situation at this time on the board of ministries. We prayed with our pastor and continued on with this pattern of changed thinking and a totally different way of pursuing the American dream.

With all of this going on in my life at this time, I found myself in the confrontation zone again, but this time I didn't feel alone. My thoughts were actually being carried out with an understanding that what I was about to stand for is the truth of the Word of God, if I planned on standing up in this conviction of drastic change.

The first approach came out of an understanding at this time of Ephesians 5:21–24. It all dealt with submitting to my husband with a trusting in God's Word to be the truth. That would not leave me alone, so I made that step by asking my husband what I should do concerning the job situation.

This was very difficult. I was so hoping he would say, "Stay and we will work it out," but a peace inside of me was weighing heavily on my heart with a trust in an unknown that I just could not put my finger on. My husband said, "I think you should come home."

I remember gasping for breath literally and while on my knees, going into a light collapse. That was not the hard step; the hard step was now walking it out. I am talking about how could I say to my boss, "I quit". And by the way, our finances are not great, and you, of all people, are aware of this since we are in the process of buying your house. All is well! I don't know how we are going to pull this off, but thanks much." I really felt like I was in a real lose-lose position mentally. But the peace continued to reside strongly within me.

Before going in the next day, I had keys to the office, so I went into the office the night before. I went into the back examination room, knelt down, and prayed, and basically the content of my prayer was, "I can't do this, Lord, but I believe You can, so I am putting my trust in You."

The next day consisted of first approaching the doctor. Once I asked if I could have a word with him before we got started, he looked at me and asked with his way of speaking, "Lillian, is everything okay?"

I answered with, "Not really." I expressed to him that there were a lot of changes going on in my life and I did not feel he should be subject to it. I was doing the best I could without having to mention the real reason I was sitting in that chair basically quitting my job.

He countered with, "Is it the pay?" He then offered me more money and also some help toward obtaining my training to become a LPN.

I felt the pressure, and the words came out, as if desperation had set in: "Doctor…, I am quitting and the Lord is leading me in this way!"

He reacted in a way that I could understand, and I will keep that private because to this day God has revealed so much to not only me but also my doctor friend. All I can say is that if I were in his shoes, I may have said worse.

He then called his wife to the back, and in their native tongue, he told her the news. She then in turn became very upset and started ordering me around with a periodic look of disdain and anger. She would then go into her native tongue. I could almost feel the cursing's she may have been speaking at that time. I asked if I could go to the bathroom, and I took my Bible discreetly in my purse. I then read Proverbs 25:21–22 from the Bible: "If thine enemy be hungry, give him bread to eat; and if be thirsty, give him water to drink. For thou shall heap coals of fire upon his head, and the LORD shall reward thee." KJV

When I came out, she started at me again without looking at me. I said her name, and she responded with, "What do you want, Lillian?" Then I opened my arms and just hugged her. I could feel her trembling and saying, "What are you doing?" I expressed that I loved her and that I was sorry.

## Homeschooling?

Now I found myself on step two of the document of change that was handed specifically to me with a purpose I didn't know then but I know now. It dealt with homeschooling. That summer I found myself at an Office Depot type of place in line with school supplies in my cart waiting my turn. As the conversations were flowing around me, they consisted of, "I am so glad these kids are going back to school. They were about to drive me crazy!" or "I don't know how much more I could take!" I stood there with that weird feeling again, as if I could not join in with the celebration of back to school! It was more like I wished that I could spend more time with them.

My husband and I starting to talk more, and I was falling in love with those out of the blue teaching moments. Our devotions were so awesome that I did not want to give them up. At this point, I went back and not only talked with first lady, but we also prayed together. After talking with my husband and him saying, "Let's do it," we then started to pursue homeschooling.

The doctor's office not only found a replacement, but it was one of the doctor's old LPNs whom he had worked with before, so there was not a great adjustment on either end in the office. I offered to train her anyway without pay, but they graciously not only kept me on for that time, but we also remained patients and good friends.

## Walking by Faith

Now we stepped into stage three, which consisted of having more children. Well, as my husband and I discussed this, it was the hardest step of all for me. You see, for years I had been saying, "Three is enough for me," and now I was reneging on it. If anyone asked why, what would I say? Well, what I ended up saying a lot, and now I say it with a boasting on my Father's ways, God directed my heart. He led us and we followed together and still do.

I found myself standing at the counter of the doctor's office that my doctor friend had referred me to, and they told me the cost of the procedure to reverse my tubal ligation. Since it was not a mandatory procedure, we would have to pay it in full. I was so happy. I was thinking to myself, *I will go home and tell my husband and we can forget about all of that* because I knew we did not have approximately $6,000 just sitting around waiting for this moment. When he said to me, "Go back," I looked at him like he was crazy. I said, "Did you hear what I said? Six thousand dollars!" He then said, "I heard you, go back and tell them to send it through the insurance anyway."

I will stop here and make comment about a suggestion that was made by Dad Thompson right before my husband took the job, and that was to check the insurance. If memory serves me correctly, his suggestion was irritating to me, but I am so glad my husband honored his dad's words, for this was when it started to pay out big dividends.

## Submit to What?

Now this was where the road got a little bumpy. The submit thing stunk so far as I am concerned at that time. Are you feeling me? I listened to his words, but before taking off with them, I said to him "You know this is my body, and I am the one who gets to choose!"

I made the appointment, walked in, and signed in. They

immediately recognized me and asked me to come to the desk. Looking at me as if I were a little off my rocker, the receptionist asked if there was anything from the last visit that was unclear to me.

I said, "No, actually my husband asked if you could just send that in and for us to continue with the services."

She then said, "You do realize that this office visit and all that is included will have to be paid by you, and this is not a covered procedure by your insurance?"

I smiled kindly and said, "Yes, I do understand what you have told me. If you could just follow through with the instructions that were given, I am sure that we will all be fine."

She then rolled her eyes and said whatever it was that she said, and that was my final interaction with the receptionist.

The doctor did the full initial exam and told me that the procedure more than likely would not succeed with a healthy pregnancy because my tubes were so badly burned. There was only a 25 percent chance of having a pregnancy at all, and he felt it was not worth the expense.

With all this being said and me going home with these types of reports, I was quiet. It was not a peaceful quiet but a slam the cabinet doors in the kitchen type of quiet. To top it off, the procedure to have my tubes undone was continuing to be scheduled. After doing the pre-op visit and the like, we got a very nasty phone call from a creditor saying very crude things over the phone concerning this $6,000 fee. My husband got on the phone and continued his debate of, "Just do what I say and we will talk later, and by the way, what was your name again?"

## Morris's Calling

During this time, my husband was also going through some changes in his life. On a Sunday morning in 1990, while the benediction was going on, after the pastor had given his sermon, he would come down out of the pulpit and would literally at times start to cry. We would call our pastor the crybaby pastor, for he had compassion for his congregation. On this particular Sunday while the pastor stood there crying out, "Come to Jesus while you still have time!" the choir was singing a song in the background, and the lyrics went something like this: "He is all I need, love is my God, I can't hold back with this love I have with thee."

At this point during the service while we were sitting in the pews, I remember my husband banging his Bible up against the pew in front of us, and he began to tremble. It took me by surprise because it was so unlike my husband to expose emotion in this very unusual way for him. He then, with tears in his eyes, went forward. During this time, he was uncharacteristically taking public transportation, leaving me with the one vehicle we possessed at that time. While riding the bus and the train into work, my husband would read his Bible every day like clockwork. He was so taken by this love of God that he became a man I had never known but I trusted him as he allowed the Lord to use him.

Even though I trusted my husband's words, my traditional ways of doing things were being violated, and I couldn't take it. I busted out of the house. I had to take a walk. This was making no sense to me, and I felt as though my life was not being considered here. I was seething with anger. I was not feeling this trusting in God thing, and I kept thinking to myself, *This is my body that they will be cutting on. Does anyone understand this?*

As I continued to walk, a strong breeze came across my face, and in the wind it seemed as though I heard the words, "I am your Doctor." What that meant I did not know, but what I can say is that it was comforting, so much so that I went back and told my husband. I kissed him and told him he was a great husband, and I trusted him as he was trusting the Lord because I knew he definitely was not trusting his bank account or the insurance company.

The very next day, we went to the hospital, and they began to prep me for surgery. While they were checking my lungs, the nurse said to me, "You have the clearest lungs I think I have ever listened to. I know you've never smoked." I agreed. After she left the room, I said, "Honey, I felt like it was okay to agree with that young lady even though I smoked for years and it hasn't been much over a year since I quit."

I felt the Lord had said to me that He had thrown that as far as the east from the west, and I knew the two would never meet. It was gone. I believed that after they put me under, I would wake up still the same because the whole time I kept waiting for the bomb to drop and for that one person to walk into the room and say, "Stop the madness." But they didn't, and we continued.

At this point in time, the church as a whole knew about what was going on with us, and they had been praying for us with the surgery and also concerning a future pregnancy. We had also prayed over the finances for the procedure. The final outcome came through a confirmation through the insurance company that the surgery would be covered 100 percent. The church was in an uproar of praise.

## A Change in Me for Real!

About four months later, we found ourselves in front of the church again with a praise report of a pregnancy. God was definitely moving in our lives. Can I share something with you? It was the best moment of my life that I will never forget. This is what happened that made all of this so real to me. Remember me going through that, "This body is mine" thing? Let me share with you an awesome moment of change that occurred in my life.

My husband and I were both in the choir. Yes, the first step to engrafting into the church! There was a certain Sunday when we were singing a song that we as the choir would enact the words by moving our arms as we sang the words. The words went like this: "They hung Him high, they stretched Him out, He hung His head, for me He died, *that's love*." I got stuck on those words, and they changed my life. I could no longer sing with the choir on the front row in the soprano section. My song went like this: "He loves me. He loves me. He loves *me*! He loves *me*!"

The pastor even stood up, turned around, raised his arms, and said with a loud voice, *"Yes!"* That was a day I will never forget ever in my life. And can I share this with you: He loves you too. All you have to do is acknowledge and think about it for a minute. Put the book down, and thank Him for loving you so much and for having such great patience with us. Remember, He gave His only begotten Son that whosoever (that's you and me) believes shall have life everlasting—life everlasting in love.

## It's too Early!

We went from ovation to great distress. I was pregnant at twenty-three weeks and going into labor. I truly thought I was being punished for all the abortions, and this was not a blessing from God. I started to condemn myself. I saw myself as being an unworthy candidate for God's work. First my water broke while I was at home on my way to help someone else who was having issues. I found myself in need of help and having issues of my own. As I hung up the phone, I felt a warm surge of water flow uncontrollably down my legs to the floor. Immediately I called my neighbor who rushed over to take me to the emergency room.

Now through all of this, my neighbor and I had a close

relationship at the time. She had just gone through an episode in her life where she had had a son. She carried him for nine months, knowing after her fourth month of pregnancy that more than likely her son would not live very long after birth due to a disease that was detected within her womb through amniocentesis. She was an amazing woman. She was a stay-at-home mom, and her husband, who is a twin, owned a landscaping business with his brother. He is a hard worker and constantly dirty. He is a great guy, and we always messed with each other, jokingly, should I say, just allowing you in on the fun.

At this time they only had one son living, and he was our son's best friend. Our relationships blossomed during these times. I remember one day her son came over to our house, and he was so excited. When he was excited, his speech became a little hard to understand, and what I thought he was saying was the Michigans were coming. Okay, I thought they must be having company coming in from Michigan. Wrong, it was the workers, and they were the Mexicans who were like family. They loved to play soccer with the boys, so that was the reason for his excitement. He also played soccer with our son on the soccer team, which caused an admiration toward my husband as coach.

My neighbor's experience gave her a different appreciation toward life that was obscure, and it intrigued me, to say the least. In her pregnancy, of course the option of termination was brought before her, and she declined. Her experience was astounding and so out of the box of the ways I thought about such things as this. What I saw being exhibited to me was a woman who was actually sacrificing this time of her life to carry a child to share only a short period of time. It was hard for me to understand. What I can say today is his name was Samuel, and even though he did not live very long, his life has impacted mine so much. I never met Samuel, but I know his name. Thank you, my dear neighbor, for sacrificing your life for a life that today I can say made a huge difference in mine. I love you, my neighbor. In God's Word it says to "Love your neighbor as yourself." Think about it.

**Surprise**

I was sent home on bed rest, and that is when my parents came. It was a great surprise. How it all came about was I believe my husband either called his parents and they in turn called my parents, who must have just thrown their clothes into the suitcase and came without question. Since we had moved, my parents only knew directions to our old house. That placed them in the hands of my walking buddy, who in turn treated them to a cup of coffee and then escorted them to our house. When my Dad peeped around the corner of the door, I went into an exuberant swelling up of uncontrollable tears. After that it took me awhile to compose myself when my mother came in, hugging me, and then in the background I heard my girlfriend in tears and in a way laughing and saying, "Aww, that is so sweet!"

My mother just jumped in without questions about what, when, why, or how come. She just slipped herself into the role I was no longer able to uphold. My mom and dad were such a blessing to us at this time. It was so amazing.

My dad one day sat on the side of my bed and just patted my hand as he looked out the window. It was a moment of great solitude even though we were sitting there together. He then got up, walked out of the room, and continued to walk out of the house. When he came back, which was some time later, he was holding a rock in his hands. He had written some words on this rock, and he then told me to hold on to this rock. To this day, even while I write this portion of this book, which I do believe was already written. I am just a tool in God's hand. I gaze to my left, and on the desk sits the rock. It says, "Jesus is the way, the truth, and the life. I *AM* resurrection." My dad is no longer here on this earth, but I thank him for sharing true life with me. And yes, I do continue to hold on to the rock that is my church home and that resides within me, carrying the Holy Spirit, who is my best friend.

Not even a couple of days had passed when, in the middle of the night, I went into labor. My life, my family members' lives, our church family our, family in Cleveland, our family at our first church, our sports families, and our world was about to take on a new face suddenly.

Chapter 5

# *What Position Do I Play?*

O ur church family was such a blessing, bringing us food, cleaning our house, and washing our clothes. Pastor and First Lady even opened their home up on the day of the suddenly delivery to take in our three children. This delivery was actually a delivery of my soul, my spirit, and especially my mind. I came to find out the love that God had for me was truly awesome and at the same time all consuming. I put it in the box of thinking known as the Ripley's believe it or not position on the shelf. Now was the time that I could choose to believe God or not if I am willing.

As my husband scooped me up off of the bed, all I could do was to just cave into his chest and try to find comfort. I could hear my mother in the background asking, "What's going on?" I could hear my husband saying, "It is time to go to the hospital, and I have to get her there as soon as possible." I heard my father's reassurance of agreement with my husband's words of direction as to what was happening and how it was to be executed. I felt my dad's hand and heard him saying, "I love you, girl."

My mother then asked if she could accompany us. At first my husband responded with a negative, until I chimed in with, "I need Mom to be with me. Please let her come." That changed the mission to a peace mode, which was taken on immediately.

I believe my husband took out the seats of the van, which allowed me to lay down in the back in my mother's arms. I could hear my mother just rambling off one prayer after another, which was comforting. Then my husband turned on the radio and pushed in a tape. The last time I was in the van, this was what I had been listening to. The song that began to play was "Hold Me" by Commissioned. At that time, even though it was the physical touch of my mother holding me, I felt a holding of security that I had never experienced before in my life. To this day when I hear that song being played, it takes me back to a time of assurance that I can always rely on, and it was the Lord God extending His hands to hold me with His Word.

When we arrived at the hospital, they took me back on a stretcher immediately since this was the hospital that had released me only a couple of days earlier. They went into the automatic mode of assessing my current status medically. I started to go into uncontrollable tremors through my body, which was confusing and disturbing at the same time. My mother continued to stay by my side. Whenever I would look her way, she would ask me, "What do you need, baby?" When she wasn't assessing me, she was praying with no shame by the window sill.

From out of nowhere, there was an urgency to either medevac me or transport me with expedience to a hospital in Baltimore. The helicopter was in use, so they had to rush me off in the ambulance. My mother was right there by my side. I did not see my husband most of the time because, being who he is, I am sure he was taking charge in areas and to some extent coaching others. Knowing my husband as I do, I believe he was watching the degrees of different characters of individuals. He would determine in his mind who to talk to and who not to talk to in order to see progress in this situation of life.

With sirens blaring, the EMTs were constantly watching the monitors and sending reports of stats and symptoms to the hospital staff. Upon our arrival, there was an immediate rush of adrenaline in the air. My mom was wonderfully assisted at this time, which made me feel more at ease. I felt like I was being introduced to different teams and then asked several questions over and over again. It became a bit redundant. I stopped answering questions.

It seemed as though a shield had come over me, and I found myself seeing mouths moving and facial features but no sound. I found myself surrounded by peace. I felt the presence of the Lord actually surrounding me. My husband had taken over with the question-and-answer sessions, and my mother chimed in when needed. I found all this out later, after the delivery.

**From Chaos to Peace**

At this time, there was a moment of peace and some sort of normalcy when my mother came over to my bed, held my hand, and asked me a question: "So, what are you going to name the baby if she's a girl or boy?" Thanks, Mom, for pulling me out of the chaos. I answered her with a very heartfelt, "If she is a girl I would like to name her after you, Mom, especially with the tie in to the biblical characteristics of Mary Elizabeth. [My mother-in-law's first name was Mary, and my mother's middle name is Elizabeth.] And if it is a boy, I will name him James Howard [James being my father-in-law's name and Howard being my dad's name]."

That was a well-received cleansing breath between scenes as my world continued to turn. Now it was time for me to find my focal point, and that came clear as I focused on His Word that had been stored up within me for such a time as this. As I set my mind on the name Mary Elizabeth, it reminded me of when Mary in the Bible had conceived, miraculously she went to see her cousin Elizabeth, who was approximately three months into her pregnancy. When they met, Elizabeth immediately knew of Mary's Immaculate Conception from the leaping in her womb. Elizabeth was expecting at a very old age, and there was a confirmation for her from her womb.

There was a moment of questions that distressed me just a little; it was concerning the viability of this pregnancy. Scenarios were being given to me on the dark side of life, such as insurance costs, the possibilities of long-term health issues, and the families that have come out of these situations with broken homes. I thought to myself, *We look to science as our god today, or should I say nature. Giving back for the sake of science to help others would probably be a viable situation.*

I am so glad the Lord did not allow me to be swayed at this time because, you see, I could have quite easily walked out of that hospital a couple of days later and started over, as some of us put it, and continued to live my life as normal. Wow, I have to think about that one, but then again, I do have life on this end today that is good and exceptional. I think I will just stay on this stage. "Script, please." Thank you, Dad.

## As My World Turns

As my world turned from the debriefing room to the delivery room, the questions turned into commands of gentle but firm words saying, "Push!" Monitors were beeping and machines moaning around me. This was definitely not your ordinary delivery. As I began to push, there really was no great difficulty in the birth process physically, but there was mentally. There were no real smiles. Faces surrounded me with concern, wonder, and doubt. When Mary was born, I distinctly remember hearing a faint cry, and that was it; she was gone in an instant. They then continued to deliver the afterbirth, clean me up, and assign me to an awaiting hospital room.

I did not have a roommate in my room. Actually, if memory serves me correctly, I believe it was a private room. I do know one thing: it was a quiet room. Every time someone came into my room, they were on the center stage of my attention.

One of the doctors came into the room. First came the reassuring handshakes of congratulations on your beautiful baby girl, and he continued with, "So, do you have a name yet?" I resounded with a bold, "Yes! Her name is Mary Elizabeth. She is named after her grandmothers." He then continued to give us the story of the rollercoaster ride that we found ourselves on. He showed us a picture of Mary and told us her Apgar levels, which were significant because, as he had stated, if she had been born by C-section, she probably would not have made it. Since she had to struggle to get through the birth canal, it gave her stronger lungs and a stronger drive to survive.

There was a story that really helped me through not only, situations like this particular scenario but through life altogether. The first one takes the rollercoaster story that the doctor gave us, which was a good way of announcing to us that we were embarking a fine line of life and death with Mary. It gives me a refreshing glass of living waters. The second one consists of the struggles that Mary went through that actually worked out for her good.

The first story starts on a plane to London, but I end up in Holland. What do I do? All of my maps and brochures help me to enjoy the beauties of Westminster Abbey and the like. What I have to do is put down the other paraphernalia and look up at the tulips, check out the windmills, and find out what Holland is all about. I know you were planning your trip for London, but let's be willing to enjoy our unchartered route here in Holland and watch this trip become one of the best trips of our lives. As we go through life, there are some turns that were not planned. Let's venture through them together, knowing that our GPS is God. He is already in our tomorrows, so let's trust in His ways, He will never leave us or forsake us.

Mary's birth was very similar to this. I was prepared for a normal nine-month delivery. That was all I ever knew. All of the clothes I had were for newborns, not preemies. Nursing my babies was a normal process, not intravenous feeding through a tube in her belly. I was used to wrapping my babies up and holding them when they cried because I am their mother and this was the natural thing to do. I was not used to listening to the sat machine scream because her tolerance levels were too low and the oxygenation in her blood was dropping. I had to put down those old brochures that I frequented after having three so-called normal births. And I had to look up and appreciate the joys of the everyday life of Mary, our miracle child.

My second story deals with the struggle that took place with Mary that reminds me of a time of talking with our oldest daughter at a very difficult time in her life. I had to release her and not feel as though my arms were the only arms that could sustain her through some tough times. I sat there looking into her eyes, holding her trembling hands. I said, "Patrice, your life is like a butterfly trying to come out of the cocoon right now. It is very difficult for me to stand back and allow you to struggle, but I know deep down inside that there are hands that are greater than mine. They are the hands that created you. I have to trust that as you struggle at this time in your life, you will come out, flying like a beautiful butterfly, but if my hands come in to manipulate the process so that in my eyes and others it looks good, you may die."

What I meant here was that without the struggle, my daughter would not be able to fly out her mission without a degree of appreciation and gratitude toward the one who created her with the abilities unless she did these things on her on. Today our oldest daughter says thank you.

## Family Roles Change

While this sudden moment was occurring in my life, the children were being taken in by our pastor and first lady. My parents were holding down the fort at home. Oddly enough, there were no streaming phone calls. It was quiet where we sat on floor number six. I found out later that the calls were streaming in at the house, and my Mom—bless her heart—was having difficulties not answering the phone. With us having an answering machine, we had instructed her that for any calls that came in that she did not know who they were, she was not responsible for those calls. When my husband returned home, he would do the callbacks with general overall information.

There were a lot of brothers and sisters at both churches, in the sports field, with my husband's job, and our surrounding neighbors, not to exclude close friends and family in Maryland and others around the states, who were interested in our situation. It kind of spread like a forest fire, as was seen by the phone calls.

My mom would still try to answer the phone as normal but with the slew of questions that were out of her realm of understanding to be able to answer, it became a bit overwhelming, to say the least.

My first time seeing Mary was that evening. My husband rolled me down in a wheelchair. It seemed to be the longest corridor I had ever gone down in my entire life. I began reciting Psalm 23:

> The Lord is my shepherd, I shall not want. He maketh me to lie down beside the still waters. [Lord, make me! I'm not there yet. Thank You

for the peace in the storm.] You restore my soul.
You leadeth me in the path of righteousness for
Your Name Sake.

I have to stop here because every time I would recite this poem, when I came to "for Your name's sake," it was emphasized greatly within me. I became emboldened when those words crossed my lips, whether physically quivering or not. Then, with a dogmatic faith, I would continue with an overriding statement of truth. "Yea, though I walk through the valley of the shadow of death, I will fear no evil."

At times while stating these words, I would very often see these blue accordion screens that were used in the rooms when a death had come to pass. I would continue, "For thou art with me; your rod and your staff they comfort me. You have prepared a table before me in the presence of my enemies: thou anointest my head with oil; my cup runneth over. Surely goodness and mercy shall follow me all the days of my life: and I will dwell in the house of the *Lord* forever. *Amen.*"

## The First Time Meeting

We got a welcome wagon of nurses who were currently working with Mary Elizabeth as we drew close to where she was stationed. Since her situation was in the high range of critical, she also had a private room. We were instructed on how to approach Mary. With a robe and mask on, we would then pull up our sleeves and take an iodine scrubber and scrub up to the elbow of our arms. This detailed washing and changing into garments went on for approximately two years after Mary came home. It was mandatory due to the high percentage of death if she were to catch anything.

There was a nurse with bright blonde hair who had the

brightest smile and bubbly personality. She was a welcome sight to a bewildered mom who really felt out of sync in my role as a mother. She gave me much reassurance while my questions started to stream concerning my daughter's condition and how to approach her without causing her any negatives to her precious life.

I felt so out of place. It was like a feeling of a surrogate mom. I felt as though the nurses knew how to handle my daughter better than I did, which put me in a bit of a funk, to be very honest.

When I approached Mary, she literally looked like a newborn baby chick. She laid there with a type of eye wrap around the top part of her head and lights on her foot connected to a long white cord. She had a beautiful head of hair and long fingers. Without any more details, I did not know how to approach my daughter. I was waiting for the nurses to tell me what to do next.

She was covered with bubble wrap, but then something caught my eye and I actually started to giggle. Her foot that was free of the needles and cords was sticking out of the plastic, so at that point I made mention to the attending nurse, who also giggled and then proceeded to put her foot back into the plastic. I then said, "Mary, are you trying to get out of there? It's okay, we will get out of here soon!"

The nurse acknowledged Mary's name and then proceeded to put her name above her bed. She wrote "Mary Elizabeth" with flowers on a pink card board. I looked at it and said to the nurse "Her name is too long for her body, so can you put under it, 'Please call me Meme'!" She said sure and gave me that big, reassuring smile and said she thought that was so cute.

## Guilt Uncovered

I found myself at a moment of revealing truths that I had been carrying around with me ever since we had left Cleveland. They were truths surrounding the aspect of the Scripture that came to mind for me before we left, and that was Jesus' sayings on the cross: "Forgive them for they know not what they do." Guilt was keeping me from forgiving them, and that enemy was in-a-me! I felt guilt that I had harbored for so long it almost seemed as though it no longer existed. It was the inner knowing of that deep, dark secret that I would not reveal to anyone until now.

The reason why is because I know Jesus came to set me in right order with the love of the hand that created me. He gave me a freedom to acknowledge myself in the eyes of the one who created me, and it caused me to no longer beat myself up but to love what He loved, and that was me.

He loved me so much that He took off His robe of righteousness for an exchange for my sins even when I did not acknowledge Him. He continued to pursue me. He paid my debts of sin and gave me and all of us a position to claim in freedom back in right order as in the beginning before there was sin and death. I now claim my right position as His bride in waiting for my Groom who art in heaven. He now has given me through His righteous blood as a sin offering a position before the Father.

What I had done was facing me on center stage and penetrating my heart. It was my sin of killing innocent lives and not just tissue, as they had told me when I had had the abortions. I found myself coming to the High Priest who is my Lord and Savior with a covering of blood, which was accepted by the Father as the spotless Lamb of God. He no longer looks at my sins. The veil has been lifted. No more are we separated. The intercourse between us is beautiful, and it continues and shall forever and ever.

I am covered by the blood of God's only begotten Son forever and ever. I now stand boldly, knowing I am the beloved and highly favored by my dad, the lover of my soul. I now can love that enemy because I can love my neighbor as myself.

So I see myself as I look out at any one person, not because of a so-called race or culture but because they are me, being forgiven, which frees me up to forgive others when their actions are pushing the Father's love away instead of drawing near. Selah. (Take some time to think on this one, and remember this: I already prayed for you before you even picked up this book. He loves you too!)

## Push Through Life

At this point I returned to my room with a battle plan in my life that did not exist just three days earlier. I had planned on nursing because as a mom that is what I was determined to do. If nothing else, this was my role as a mom to Mary at this time, and I was going to do the best I could in my position with a function that I considered was designed by God specifically for Mary, with a special order. I was ready with milk to deliver.

I met the La Leche nurse on the floor, and she introduced me to my new friend the pumping machine. Believe me when I tell you this: I used that thing like it was a religion to be practiced with a great degree of timing.

I would drink the proper amounts of fluids and eat the foods that would naturally produce what was needed for Mary's growth and health. The nurse was pleasantly surprised to see the progress in such a short period of time. It was good because the first milk that comes in is called colostrum. It is of a thick consistency and has high levels of good stuff, especially in the case of a premature birth. The only thing: it had to be used freshly, so all excess had to be thrown out. I became the gestapo of breast milk, making sure the nurses knew there was milk always available for Mary.

As the milk changed its consistency, it became safe to store it in the freezer. They had a designated freezer outside the pumping room that was convenient for all nursing moms. We each had a section. Needless to say, the freezer mainly had Mary's milk in there, but I did keep abreast of the milk situation daily.

After familiarizing myself with my position to play within the hospital walls, I was introduced to Mary's caretakers and their individual roles in her care, such as the radiologist and the respiratory therapists, which we became very close due to the intense care with oxygen that Mary needed. The fellow on board was Dr. Gewald, who was a great doctor. There was also Dr. Vescardi, who we fell in love with. She said, "Who knows, Meme may become a neonatal surgeon." And she still can Dr. V! We became acquainted with their staff and the ways they carried out the individual care plans, understanding that this was not only a hospital but it was a university hospital. With that understanding, there were students who would do rounds with the doctors for learning purposes.

**Every Day Is Enjoyed**

I also joined the NICU families counseling session, which was interesting as we sat and shared our individual situations. There were some who were in a unit called the step-down unit, and they were approaching their dismissal from the hospital.

When it came time for me to introduce myself, I felt myself seething inside due to the fact that out of the three or four individuals who talked, the only good report was a date of departure. The reason for my overwhelming reaction at this time was due to the fact that deep down inside, with the extremities of Mary's case, I knew we might not be reaching the step-down unit. So I answered like this: "Hello, my name is Lillian Thompson. My daughter's name is Mary. She is named after her grandmothers. It was brought to my attention that she is one of their smallest births of survival at this time at 480 grams; they say she is like a sandwich without the meat in comparison to her weight. She is now doing quite well. She is a fighter with a strong drive to live. I am happy to celebrate this time right now because, every moment, every second I am finding myself celebrating life not only for my daughter but for myself. I don't know the day or the hour, so I say with gratitude, 'Happy day, happy hour, happy minute,' all to be celebrated."

I felt very foreign in this bunch because it seemed like the room was set up to complain about what went wrong or to say, "I am finally getting out." I could not join in. As a matter of fact, I did not join the group. It was not a good thing for me at the time, so I chose not to return for the betterment of us all.

We still greeted each other in the hallway and talked if we crossed each other's paths and the moment was available, with sincere hearts corresponding as we all continued on our individual paths of life. I can say most of our extended relationships with other parents in the NICU occurred as the moments of life presented themselves before us and we reacted on the spot in prayer and hugs and phone calls late in the evenings, with understanding hearts on the other line that we would not have to go through great deals of explanations for the listener to be on board at a time when all that was needed was a place to deposit some real, deep pain and have it received with prayer and hope, believing that God loved us all. There really was no consideration toward race in this realm because there was the daily acknowledgment of death surrounding the unit, which had no respecter of persons.

### Would You Like a Ride?

A funny thing happened on my first trip home. I guess you're thinking, *This doesn't seem to be a moment of laughter,* but oh yes, my husband knew that even in times like these, we can make jokes. Well, I don't believe he was trying to make jokes, but as I write these words out to you today, it seems like a funny joke. Yes, I was literally looking for the candid camera.

My husband is a very systematic individual, so first he wanted to make sure that all matters that needed to be closed out on my end of signing and details of parking passes were taken care of since we would be returning not just once but sometimes several times in a day. Please remember that we have a forty-five- to sixty-minute commute one way to and from the hospital with no delays on a good day on Route 50. Anyone who is familiar with this area will take this well-emphasized tidbit with great appreciation to its importance. The rest of you, when visiting Baltimore, Maryland, these words I will announce for you to heed.

My husband ironed out all of the wrinkles, and it was now time for us to leave. We had all of the contact numbers for all stations in play position involving Mary's care. Remember, my husband is a coach at heart, and he plays his role well, to say the least. Seeing that all things were settled, he proceeded to go and get our van. The nurse then took me down to the front door for departure.

As I sat at the door waiting for my husband to come, there was another woman also departing at the same time. We started conversing, and she said to me, "Hey, I remember you. I think we came in at the same time." At this point in time, I was trying to figure out how this could be with me coming in by ambulance. At the same time, my husband pulled up, said hello, and continued to take all of my items and place them in the car. Well I then asked the woman how her baby was doing. I believe she had a boy, and she responded positively. I then proceeded to tell her that I would pray for her and her son because there was some sort of disconnection that she had shared with us concerning the father of her son.

Now mind you, I was going through a difficult transition, but it was refreshing to be able to share with others a ray of hope. As my husband was helping me into the van, she commented on us having a nice van. I said thank you, and as I positioned myself to say good-bye, my husband asked her if she needed a ride, and she accepted the ride! Now in my head I was thinking, *Selfishly, of course.* This was to be my personal moment of tears and emotion—no, not so much.

I had my new friend sitting behind me giving my husband directions over my shoulder around downtown Baltimore. It got to the point that I felt a little uncomfortable, to say the least, because she would tell us to go one way, and then she would change her mind and say, "Naw, let's just make a right here, and then a left at the next corner." Now my patience was running thin, and I give my husband the *look*. He then said, "Hopefully we have gotten you closer, and you should have no problems getting home."

She started to get her things together, thanked us, and proceeded to depart from the van. It's a little funny now, but as we think about it, here was a life who had given life and where was the acknowledgment? My husband and I, having a family at home, not only acknowledging a life but sharing this life experience with me, and this woman, it seemed, was out of sorts in the same arena. Hopefully she was telling us the truth, because I must say I never saw her again, but this situation did cause an impact of hurt and now even some laughter.

After we dropped the woman off, I asked my husband what caused him to do that because normally this just was not like him. He had no real explanation, so we tossed it up to God's candid camera moment of our lives. Hopefully it brought on a laugh for our Father and thoughts to capture for us.

Chapter 6

# The Great Awakening

As our roles took on change in our family, it seemed as though everyone had already been given the script. We had our praying brothers and sisters. There was one sister who came to our house who I will never forget. I was comfortable offering food or water because either my mother had fixed something or there was something that came in abundance for the day.

During her visit, this young lady was different. She may have had a cup of water, but after that she started asking me how I would like certain cleaning details done in the house, like, "Do you prefer your bathrooms to be cleaned with a cloth or paper towels?" This went on for a while, as she proceeded to ask me what days would be best within the times she had available to come out and clean my house without pay. I was shocked, and this was such a blessing also for me and my mom. We arranged the times, and not only did she clean the house, but she also would take our clothes and wash them and bring them back all folded! It was amazing, to say the least. She also made the best homemade rolls—well, other than my mom's, of course.

She did teach me how to bake those delectable treats that even won my mom's approval. She and I remained closely knitted until we moved from Maryland. These were the types of encounters that we were finding ourselves in almost daily. At times it was a little overwhelming.

I remember when our pastor let me know that he had gone to see Mary and it was difficult for him. He expressed to me that it hurt him to see such a tiny life with all the needles and wires surrounding her. I thanked him, for as this was going on in our lives, our church had started to take off in memberships. For him to take the time out of his day to come out and see Mary even though she didn't know he was there was a very delicate moment. He was recognized, and also all the others, by the one who continues to smile on them. Thank you, Pastor, we love you!

When we do things out of the goodness of our hearts because we are moved to do it, even though there is no big fanfare, God sees all of those moments. I believe He smiles down on us at those times. Thank you all, and may God continue to bless you here on earth as it is in heaven, even with all that surrounded us in this journey you all aided in an experience that caused us to see heaven in action.

So far as the sports activities, this is when carpooling became a blessing in the wings. Our other three children continued in their sports, and in some ways I still don't know how my husband continued to coach. I believe in ways it was like a normal outlet that was in position for him to plug himself right into without thought.

My parents stayed with us for approximately six weeks. When they had to leave, it was very hard, but they did have another home, and if memory serves me correctly, one time my father had to go home, and he left and Mom stayed. It really was surreal. Everything was so well taken care of that my concentration on the hospital details was a lot easier to take on, as well as my new role as stay-at-hospital mom and stay-at-home mom.

**Honor Your Parents; It Pays**

As for my husband, he continued plugging along at work. His coworkers were a blessing to us during this time. There is one thing I cannot forget concerning my husband's job. Do you remember when he took the job and his dad continued to bear down on the point of insurance? It kind of irritated me. Well, because of my husband's dogmatic temperament while handling irritating yet well-deserved situations, our insurance comes into play here.

My husband is the one who can give specific details, but bottom line, in the end Mary's care was, needless to say, in the millions. If memory serves me correctly, her bill came in an expanding brown envelope. The last dollar amount I saw that had by it "you owe" was at least $700,000 dollars. In the end, our insurance bill turned out to be $0. I have the final card to prove it. Even though your parents' words may seem a little outdated and off center, honor them. You just don't know where those words being honored will place you in the end. The Lord's words are to be held as truths in all things, and it is because He loves us.

**All Things Work Together for Good**

There were a couple of instances during our ten-month stay at UMMS that put me in position of recognizing a true and living God who loved me.

First of all, God took my attention off of Mary's condition and started redirecting my attention toward the nurses, doctors, and therapists. They were all individuals to be noticed who were on the edge of life and death more so than even Mary.

In the beginning of our visits, I would sit and read to Mary these children's books that were filled with the Word. One story that moved me greatly was *Benjamin Bumblebee and the Giant Tumbleweed* from the Christian Mother Goose treasury.

In the rhyme, there is a bumblebee by the name of Benjamin. He starts out his journey with the same verse that he ends his journey with. The verse says, "All things work together for good for those who love the Lord." While he is continuing to speak this verse out loud, he finds himself in diverse situations. First he ends up in a tumbleweed, which makes it so he is in no longer in control as to where he goes or how fast. It is all up to the tumbleweed. As he continues his journey in a high wind storm, he ends up helping others, and in the end he states with a strong resolution, "All things do work together for good."

As I read that rhyme today, my heart leaps with an understanding as to how I felt toward it then. Looking at it today, I stand with a knowing in the fact that all things do work together for good, and my Father is the same yesterday, today, and forever more.

As I continued to visit Mary, I met a couple of people whose children had passed away. It was very sad, but my mission was with the parents and where they were in relation with the Father knowing that they could make a decision with their lives also. I really did care.

I also came to a resolution as to the children's passing, knowing deep down inside that death was no respecter of persons, meaning the shoe could be on the other foot. I linked this to the Word of God, which states that we are all born in sin. My question was, what about the children? When they pass, do they go to hell? That did not seem right, so I went to our Bible study at the church. Our senior pastor answered my question with the story of David and his first son and that the Lord had revealed to him his child being carried in the arms of the Lord. With my tenacious spirit, I did not stop there. I continued to search, and the Lord made it very clear to me that if a child cannot make a right-minded decision as to what was right or what was wrong, it was not held against him.

I then went out not only into the NICU but also by request onto the floor where there were trauma pregnancies. I felt like Benjamin from the nursery rhymes failing to see due to the clouded perspectives with the whirlwinds of life that it was the Lord who was using me even though my trials were continuing to be played out. Mary's life was continuing with death threats almost daily as Meme's health and well-being were being attacked. She was not tolerating being taken off the oxygen, which caused her to be on oxygen for almost two years. She had several veins blown, which made burn marks on her body. She had several surgeries, such as hernia removal, spinal tap, and many others that I cannot recall. There were many callings to my life. But as I continued to walk through those halls, I chose a calling, which was a love toward my neighbor as myself with the Shepherd's prayer on my lips and a word of, "All things work together for good for those who love the Lord." It was all good.

Thanks, Dad, for continuing to hold on to us even when we don't want to be held I believe that is when you hold us even tighter.

## Someone's Always Watching

I found out from the respiratory therapists that they were observing me when I was with Mary reading. They came to a conclusion that her saturation levels tended to be higher at those times. She was tolerating her oxygen levels. Their suggestions were for me to make a tape recording of my voice reading the book to Mary so that when I was not there, it would help her to stay in a calmer state of mind.

The reading I would do with Mary was implemented on to her care plan by the respiratory therapists. On occasions of meltdown, not only did these readings seem to keep Mary's position at peace, but it was ministering to me also in my new role. After doing this, they made a note on her isolette stating that the tape was to be played for Mary's moments of desaturation.

What I neglected to tell them was that the only tape that I could find at home to use was a tape from our church with one of our pastor's sermons. Well, with that buildup, I walked into the room one day, and Mary's saturation levels were at 100 to 98. I was so excited to see this, especially since her ranges were normally hovering at around 75 to 82 on a good day.

I approached Mary's isolette, and I could hear a male voice with extreme volume in her space. I opened her side door, and immediately I recognized the voice. It was our pastor's, and obviously she was enjoying the message! What struck me as strange and made me giggle a little was that the nurses had made it clear to me that around preemies in this fragile stage of life you are to use a very calm, peaceful range of communication because they feed off of their surroundings, which is known to be true. Well, this was not calm, and if you knew our pastor, his range can escalate, and not only that, it can stay there for a while, to say the least.

What I saw with Mary was her sensitivity to the Word of God. Wow! I was amazed to say the least. I also was moved in a way of trusting God's Word on a different level with this new revelation that was revealed to me personally. I respect our doctors who are constantly in practice mode, but there is a Doctor who spoke to me in the winds. He has confirmed to me that He is finished and His Word is true and can be trusted. He was once again surgically removing a form of doubt that resided within me.

## Whose Words Do I Believe?

One day after this occasion, while at home I received a call from the hospital stating that Mary's condition was to the degree of, as they put it, "We can have a priest here to give last rites!" I had no idea what that meant other than my daughter was dying!

I frantically made my way to the hospital. Almost the entire time my thoughts were focused on death. I started to think about the blue screen that I might encounter. At one point in time, I did become distracted by the traffic as several people were cutting me off or racing with me with a mentality of trying to be first, which was frustrating, to say the least. It did cause me to think a little out of the box, taking into consideration the ways I choose to drive when someone is driving at a pace that is a little faster than the rest that maybe, just maybe, they got a call and need to be wherever their unexpected situation has arisen.

Also this was before cell phones, so it is a little different today having direct verbal access at all times unless we are out of zone. Sorry for the tangent—obviously I felt that it mattered because it changed a mental habit I had while driving without thought.

As I approached the hospital after parking my van in the garage, which was right across the street from the hospital, I proceeded quickly to the hospital. While approaching the street that I had to cross, I found myself to be very anxious and weary while pushing the button on the pole designed to force the signal light to red for those who were waiting to cross the street. When the light turned red, I immediately started my dash, and a woman grabbed my shoulder and said to me, "It's okay. Everything will be all right" She released me, and I continued to cross the street. After crossing, I took a quick glance over my shoulder to see this lady to see if I knew her. Understand where my head was right then. I felt like I was grasping at the wind, with no real anchor other than death. I had never seen this lady before, and I had no idea who she was. As I searched ever so quickly, there were no signs of this lady anywhere. I chalk this one up to angels. I don't know if you believe in angels or not, but after that encounter I did, and I still do.

As I approached the floor, it was like an automatic pilot from within me that would cause me to go into Psalm 23 "The Lord is my shepherd." While I was entering the final doors, a nurse interrupted my steps and gave me a smile and a report that put out my fire of anxiety. She said, "Mary has come around, and she is doing great. Are you okay?" With that I basically collapsed in her arms with a, "Praise the Lord!"

## No Matter What

One of the final transformations that occurred during my journey of life was major—so major I believe this was and is the great turning point in my life, giving me a peace that surpassed all of my understanding. As we approach this part of the ride, please make sure your seatbelts are secure, for this drop is major.

It all begins on a typical day in the NICU. No extremes were occurring on the floor that need added attention. I came in, as was normal. Actually the Scripture that continued to lead me was Psalm 23: "in His name's sake." I continued to walk. By now I had quite an eclectic compilation of books, all containing Scripture in child-related scenarios of life. There was one thing that I had come to understand in going to the library. I really had to do an in-depth search for these types of books, which put me on a trail that led back to that desire of teaching, which has been my heart's desire ever since I was a little girl.

This bag of books that I acquired was a very large canvas Disney character bag with metal handles. I placed the bag up in the window sill and once again thanked my Dad for His presence. Of course I had already taken on the rituals of the washing of hands and having proper covering with a mask on, which by now was not as cumbersome as it was in the beginning of the journey.

Mary seemed to be pretty settled. Her sats were ranging around 85, which for Mary now was considered a norm, not to be alarmed. I asked the attending nurse for the overnight report from the night shift, and it had been a quiet evening with no episodes. I then opened Mary's little porthole and said, "Good morning, Meme, Mommy's here!" I then continued to talk to Meme, as was normal for us to do. I would sit down with the bag on the floor by my feet, and I'd tell her about some of the books I had specifically picked out for not only her but for Mommy also.

I proceeded to read to her as normal, and then it happened— the suddenly unexpected moment of ridiculous change from normal into frenzy and mayhem. Her saturation machine started to scream, which also became a norm because sometimes it would be misplaced on her foot. At this point I calmly reached up to turn it off, and I looked over at the attending nurse. At this point we had a comfortable relationship with Mary's care. She attentively looked over and reassured me that everything should be okay as she completed what she was doing as she was tending with another child in the NICU. All of a sudden Mary's sats showed 56 and dropping as if this was an accurate read. The nurse now was at the isolette checking Mary out from the other side, reaching in the opposite porthole.

All of a sudden, with a very direct order and without any hesitancy, the nurse asked me to please leave the room as two other nurses entered the room. I went out of the room immediately to stand on the outside and proceeded to watch on from the window with a hope that all things were going to settle down soon. Multiple doctors entered, and at this point I visually could no longer see my little Meme.

Oh my goodness! I realized that I had left the bag by

the isolette. Then I could feel my milk coming in from the excitement, and I needed to express it, but my portable pump was by the bed with my bags. I looked around to see if there was anyone I could ask to go in to retrieve my bags, and I realized everyone was now in the room. I needed my bag.

*This makes no sense,* I thought to myself. *Let me just go in there and get my stuff.* So I went in and no one noticed my entry because of the intensity of the moment. I reached in, and there was a sudden break in the crowd. They realized that it was me, and the immediate reaction of panic I saw set in. I then expressed in a very peaceful way, "Please continue, your hands are being used now." As I reached for my bags, I did get a glimpse of my little Meme. They were flipping her, and she was all purple. She no longer looked like life. I actually felt myself staring death in the face.

I do know how I proceeded; I just cannot explain it. I hope this makes some type of sense. At times things I encountered during this period of my life, I found myself truly dependent on what I could not see, but I continued with a hope that was beyond all measure. Yes, I found myself actually walking by faith and truly not by sight. Let us continue the ride. I know at times it may be a little uncomfortable, but proceed with the caution of love that stands at the end ready to help us at our time of need.

I then found the secretary who was stationed in the unit, or it may have been that she actually found me. I expressed to her my need to go to the pumping room, which had an entry key that once the room was in use, no one else could enter until the keys were returned. The keys were available, so I thanked her and proceeded to the crying room—oops, I mean the pumping room.

With all that being said, you know what occurred to the extreme after I contained myself enough to continue to the room. The tears began to flow nonstop, and at the same time, so did my milk. I ended up pumping about thirty-two ounces of milk! I prepared two bags for the freezer, but then all of a sudden it all seemed nonsensical, and I proceeded to pour the milk down the drain. I then remember saying to myself, "What sense does this all make anyway?"

My senses were now taking control, and I felt as though I was spiraling down into a deep seat of defeat and devastation. It was at this point I felt a quiet presence from within, and it was directing me in a weird type of way. I was willing because to be honest I did not care. I was actually casting my care over to this soft voice that instructed me to praise Him, not for what He does but for who He is, regardless. It doesn't matter anymore. "Lord," I said, "Hallelujah." I continued to repeat this one word. It started out very faint, and it then increased. I started to regain my strength, and there was a definite renewal within me.

I then proceeded to clean my face with the available tissues, and if memory serves me correctly, I did use them all. I cleaned up my pumping equipment and returned it to its rightful resting place, and I prepared myself to walk out of that door. As I turned the handle, I did not feel quite the same as I felt when I had entered.

There is an old saying about certain individuals who never found themselves in any trouble. It was said that they were like a well-greased skillet where nothing could stick to them. I felt like a blood-covered child of the King of Kings, and nothing was going to move me from my faith and belief in His Word, no matter what! I was covered in love.

As I opened the door, I felt as though I was on a mission and the controls were no longer in my hands. I was so comfortable with my new position. I continued down the hall, and by this time the screen was in the room. I handed the keys to the secretary, and she came from behind the desk to give me a hug.

I returned the favor, and then one of the nurses approached me and asked me of what faith I was. I answered with, "Baptist." Then she asked me if I wanted to call my pastor, and I responded confidently with a resounding, "No, as a matter of fact I already called my Father, and His line is never busy. I'm good, thank you so much. Please continue to allow your hands to be used, and I will be back."

She looked at me as if she were a little bewildered and said, "I really believe that you should stay due to how serious the situation is at this point." I responded with a confident, "All things are going to work together for good. I trust Him."

## The Eyes of the Lord

Now the secretary had a justifiable reason to be in the state of mind. She was in understanding the situation that was being addressed and the average response from a parent, especially one who spent so much time on the floor. I assure you that with this situation, as with many others in this realm of sensitivity of life and death, not only with just our case but many others the doctors, nurses, therapists, and counselors, I can say in the end we came to a sound agreement that all things did work together for good. I continued to find myself alone in the car, with no cell phone, so there was no access for anyone to call me or for me to call them at this point. To this day, how I made it home is a mystery. I did physically, but mentally I was gone.

As I was driving home, I did have an interesting period that I do recall that was very penetrating and very real. While I was driving with the constant tearing over my vision, there was a moment when I looked up, and it was as if I were looking into the eyes of love that were cutting down into my very being. It was a moment of me acknowledging eyes of Love with an intense look with directions for me to continue and that I was not alone.

When I drove up the driveway and parked the van, it was as if I were watching another individual's life story being played out. I was intensely watching. I made it upstairs to our bedroom. I was alone but not really; peace was there, and I was ready to fall into His arms. The children were in school, and the house was quiet. The bedroom was as I had left it, with the curtains drawn shut, and it was dark. I fell prostrate on the floor, literally in reverence as unto God my Father, not in want of anything other than rest and assurance.

I was at rest, and at this very moment is when the phone started ringing. I did not move, I just lay there, and then I heard the automated voice of the answering machine, followed by the beeps. Then I heard the attending doctor's voice. With excitement he was expressing to me that obviously I had not made it home yet, but he wanted to let me know that Mary was back, and her sats were now rising. He was obviously watching the monitor, because he then said her sats were at 89, no 92—she looks great! At that point I raised up off the floor, and I found myself now in a kneeling position with my arms raised high. I just started to cry and say, "Thank You, Father, thank You!" This continued for some time. There were no time restraints with this time of praise that was continual.

I did finally call the hospital, and they encouraged me to rest and to be reassured that Mary was looking great. They were greatly pleased with her turn around. Only those attending would be able to relate their extreme personal celebrations about what happened that day. I only heard bits and pieces when they shared them with me. That was for them and the loving eyes that kept me as I drove home.

That evening I found myself at the church. It had to be a Tuesday night, for that is when Bible study would be held, and I believe it still is. As I went into the church, I could hear the praise songs from the congregation that was gathered at this time. I quietly found a seat and sat for a moment, once again saying, "Thank You, Father." I then stood up and raised my hands high above my head, and there was a shout like I had never experienced before. I then opened my eyes, and as I looked toward the pulpit, Pastor was mouthing the words, "Why are you here?"

It was as if I was answering him internally as a smile came across my face, giving him his answer as I raised my hands again, and then I continued until it was time for me to go. I was now on a different time schedule. It was not with the traditional ways of doing things not in disturbance but with a grace covering of peace.

## Civil Duties

As I found myself so heavily entrenched in my situation, I also had to take on my civil duty relative to elections. This was an election year, and there were two candidates. One was for the Democratic Party, and the other was for the Republican Party. Now traditionally I would vote without thought because I just felt as though it was right to vote Democrat. In families surrounding me traditionally, it was just something that was done, or so I thought, because I did not start voting until I was married.

The Word of God started to be the standard of truth to be respected as the final of all things considered. I found myself at a crossroads with tradition and truth, and truth now won in my heart and mind regardless, of how I felt. "What does the Word say?" The end.

So I voted as the Word says, not as I used to, traditionally without thought, provoking thought generationally instead of traditionally. This also was a critical time in my household. It was starting to look very different as to the world's ways of doing things. The questions began. I asked myself, "Are you becoming an Abolitionist toward the slavery institution of traditional thinking?" I believe the answer was yes!

I found myself running away from my traditional ways of thinking that had been acceptable in the groupthink of worldviews outside of the biblical worldview. I have to be very honest—this was an awkward step in my life that I had a peace with because of the position I stood in. Feeling and knowing for myself the grace that had been displayed before my eyes of Christ standing in front of me saying, "Put all charges on Me, and let her go in peace." It was a peace that surpassed all of my own understandings. It was not a path that was heavily traveled, so I took the lesser, and it made all the difference in my life. Jesus said He came so that we could have peace not like the world gives but such as He had. He gave it to us if we want it.

As for me, I say, "So be it unto me," and thank You, Father, for sending Your Son as a love letter to me.

Chapter 7

# Where Is Your Faith?

*I found myself walking in a* confidence not in me but in a trusting in the Word of God as being the standard of my life with all decisions. What I found out continually was that His Word is the truth, and the truth was setting me free on a daily basis. A lot of my bondages were actually mental, not physical. As a man thinketh, so is he, or she in my case. When I go out in the mornings, it is my habit to pray, "This is the day that the Lord has made, and I will rejoice in it." I asked myself, "How can I rejoice in it if I don't have the confidence in His Word, which states that He made the day and that He made me?" And it was all done in order with purpose.

Now let us set everything into cruise control. Mary started to gain weight. Her care began to be not as critical. There was a feeling that we were coming out of the woods. I continued to come in and read to her daily, as was the norm at this point. One of my celebration days that I will share started with Mary's attending nurse, who had good news for me after six weeks. "Mom today you can finally hold your baby girl!" What? Okay, this took a transition of the thoughts into something unexpected but so gratifying.

The first hold consisted of a help in her bathing. I actually arranged for her siblings to come in and join in with her bathing ritual. It was such a great moment. The next holding came with an attempt to nurse, or should I say breastfeed, it was difficult for her to latch on. However, just having her that close, feeling her heartbeat and her breathing, added life to my life. It was essential to her growth. They called it a kangaroo pouch type of hold, which eventually would lead to nursing.

Even the children were starting to come in more often to visit and do their homework while in the lounge area when it was not in use. Everything was moving along quite well. There were a few bumps here and there but nothing major to cause any disorder.

We were no longer attending services at church. I guess you can say the hospital became our church. I found myself encouraging a few families here and there. It was actually encouraging for me. One couple had twins, and they were from Ghana. One of the twins passed, and I was there when it occurred. Through this time, our relationship grew to the point that it reached outside of the doors of the hospital before Mary came home. It was awesome taking the children to their home. After their son came home, we celebrated with them with a traditional meal from their homeland. It was really cool. They were in their traditional garments, and we had a wonderful time. That was the first time I had ever tasted plantains. They were good. They tasted like a bland banana. It was a hope-filled time of celebrations of life shared between us. All our children even jelled without any real prompting. What a great day of hope!

## We Are One

I remember watching their son grow by leaps and bounds before they left the hospital. It was so exciting seeing them go from a grievous situation to a celebration of life. At times I must say it did strike me as strange how so many babies were coming and going quickly. We were becoming the story that everyone can tell because we were known not only because of the severity of Mary's condition in the beginning but because we also now fell into the bracket of longtime residents. It was even brought to our attention for Mary to be transferred once they would get her out of the woods to be moved to the Ronald McDonald house, which was the house of long-term care. That to me again was almost like saying she was going to stay critical for the rest of her life. At that time I was not willing to agree with a quick judgment call.

I carried a calendar every day, and in it I recorded the details of Mary's care, with many praise reports of her successes. I used it as a tool of encouragement to moms and dads and sometimes those outside of the hospital, like the grocery store attendant who aided me with my groceries. I would share with family and friends as they would come to visit. It was a good tool to share and prepare visitors before going out to the hospital to visit. It was used to enlighten their understanding, seeing that this would not be a normal baby in the nursery visit.

This was a regular baby book. It had stickers in it like, "Baby's first haircut," which was when Mary received her first IV in her head because that was where they could locate the best vein. "Baby's first solid foods" became Mary's feeding tube in a bag taped on that day.

As these things continued on the sixth floor, one day I was called to the phone in the room. I had never gotten a call in the room, so it seemed to me to be a little out of the ordinary. When I answered, on the other end of the line was a very kind female voice. She made references to why she was calling me— to provide some private counseling sessions. The way I was handling Mary's case was so rare that she just wanted to spend some time with me to talk. I told her that I would talk with my husband about this and then we could go from there. She then almost immediately responded with, "Mrs. Thompson, this service does not involve your husband, so there's no need for any external individuals to be involved." She also expressed that it would be a few private sessions just between her and myself.

This was a red flag of caution for me because, as I responded to her, there was nothing done that I would not share with my husband, for he and I are one. She still proceeded to set a date, and on that day that she had scheduled without an agreement from me, she showed up, came into the room with me, and introduced herself as the hospital's psychiatrist. Okay! I was a little on edge, but it was all good. In my mind I was saying, "Let's go, girlfriend!"

She began with a questioning survey on how I had been holding up with Mary's extreme care, which was a little out of the norm. Her stay had been longer than first anticipated, and her weight gain was not progressing in a normal fashion for preemies. She just wanted to know how I was handling all of these shortcomings as Mary's care continued to be addressed at the hospital.

I began to express my faith to her, and she looked at me as if I were speaking a different language. Then she asked her big question: "What if your God does not come through?"

My response was, "He already has, and no matter what I would continue to trust in His Word. As for Mary, I celebrate each day of life that God allows for me to have with her."

But it was not Mary that I was concerned with. It was actually those surrounding me, such as the psychiatrist. My concerns were toward those who could make an intelligent decision with their individual lives. Her attitude was very belittling toward my faith, which was fine because at this point she became another opportunity to bring before my Father.

Of course, after this my husband was aware of this situation, so his antenna was up and beeping. Going into the next week, Mary had a crash that was pretty serious, so my attentions were a little more absorbed into what was going on in her surroundings.

Well of course, wouldn't you know, I forgot about the scheduled appointment that was not agreed upon again. It came at a very untimely moment as far as the way I was feeling at this time of change in Mary's condition. The phone rang, and the nurse answered. Then she gestured for me to come and answer because the call was for me.

I answered and heard the psychiatrist's voice. In her voice I personally felt a condemning deep down in my soul. The words spoken were gnawing on my nerves, with her next set of biting questions that I didn't want to hear or answer at this time. While holding the phone, with a weariness in my heart, I heard her say, "How are you handling things? I got the report on Mary's turnaround. Are you okay?"

I told her I really felt like this was not the best of times, and her response was "Actually this is perfect timing because now is the time you should talk out your feelings. Since I'm here, I'll be right up!"

I was aching inside at this point. I prayed, "Okay, now is the time I have to confront this situation, but Lord, how much of this am I supposed to bear? Because right now I feel like striking out in anger or just sitting there like a dirty rug ready to be struck and give up the dust. Right now I am trusting in the Word that says when I am weak You are strong, Father."

I stepped out of the room and proceeded to strip myself of the visiting garments with a snatching motion, and then I balled them up and tossed them into the receptacle.

I had a vehement attitude of unwillingness to meet with her, but I continued to make the steps of faith. I heard her heels with a stride of confidence and a condescending smile. I slowly began to walk her way, and then all of a sudden what did I see but yes! It was my husband, my superman! Now my stride became stronger as I approached my friend, and of course my husband had no idea that this was the psychiatrist I had talked with him about. He was curious and wanted to talk to her just as much or maybe even more than she wanted to talk to me.

So the smile on my face she thought was a greeting to her presence in all actuality was because of the man who was coming up behind her. She stopped to open the door to the pumping/meeting room. And as she gestured for us to enter, I said, "Hi, honey, it is so good to see you!" with a brief kiss and embrace that I truly needed at this time.

I then introduced the now-shocked individual to my husband, and she shook hands with him and then proceeded to explain to my husband that if he would like, since Mary was the one that he obviously came to see, he could go on and do that because "This session was just for your wife, not you. I'm sorry." My husband's response was the same as mine, "Whatever you have to say to my wife, you can say it to me also, for we are one. If you can't do that in that order, then I guess you will not be talking with my wife."

At this point, it was set on her table of response, so she grudgingly accepted the proposition we made. As we sat in the room, it was my husband's questions that overwhelmed the psychiatrist to the point that all sessions—however many they were going to be—were canceled at that point.

To the psychiatrist, I thank you for your measures of truly trying to help out. It caused a little confusion on your end but peace on mine, and I do believe you got the final report. My prayer is that it brought a peace for you also and maybe even a smile.

What was being questioned was my faith. It was causing so much attention that it caused an order to be put in place for a psychiatrist to research an area that obviously was not the norm.

Remember, as we continue to make those steps of faith, even when it seems like we are not ready for this one, your steps are ordered by the Lord, the one who knew you were going to be in this position before you even found yourself in it. It says in His Word that before this world was made He had ordered our steps, and I do believe the Word of God. And those steps are not just for you but others surrounding you.

## I Just Want to Help

One day I walked in to visit with Mary, and as I approached her isolette, there was a foreign object hanging inside. It was a crystal. The nurse who took it upon herself to do this was trying to help. I understood what was meant behind the action, so it did not anger or agitate me. It was just another opportunity to confront in love.

Since she saw my faith being exhibited, this was her way of contributing to Mary's healing. The nurse expressed to me that the crystal was there to aid in the healing for Mary's lungs.

I did take the crystal out of Mary's isolette because my faith was not toward God's attributes with what He had created. The nurse didn't stand in the position I stood in to consciously acknowledge Him and how He created me in His image and not an object.

I take this time to acknowledge Him as Creator and Savior of us all. I was truly trusting in Him and Him alone. I also expressed that with the nurse with a matter of fact statement of, "Let's just trust Him, the one who created the stone and the one who created us to acknowledge His hand in life." Let's do this!

This nurse was willing, but there were some things that she was holding onto. I could tell by her words to me as we were approaching the time of Mary's departure. What she said was that from what she saw in the physical of Mary's condition, her weight was not at regulation for departure. She was still depending on oxygen, and at this time she would still have some little episodes. What she said was, "She will be back, take my word on this one." I retorted with a confident, "I don't think so, but thanks for your judgment of Mary's assessment at this time."

## Can We Do This?

Mary did eventually come home after eight months. Before her departure, there were several meetings set to get us ready for the departure and the external care that would be needed in order for her to come home. I had no idea what in-home nursing care meant. I know the way it sounded as they explained it, and I started to feel like we were about to be invaded by in-home nurses I did not know, and they did not know Mary.

While my anxieties started to kick in, our counselor was great as she continued to encourage me in the knowledge that my husband and I carried because of the time spent with Mary there in the hospital. Even the doctors gave us a strong thumb's-up because we were not walking out the door in ignorance. With all that being said, there was a great attachment that was created during our stay at the hospital. As the tree was growing, it started out with straps for support and those straps were the doctors, nurses, therapists, and even the garage attendant. Now it was time to cut those straps and allow the tree to grow.

When we received this news, it was with an excitement that now was the time. I found myself at home preparing for the new arrival. I also realized that my life had been absent from home for the last eight months. I'd been there physically but not mentally. I totally missed my other children's activities, whether at school or with the extracurricular activities. Guilt tried to set in, but everything was moving so fast that it really had no place to sit.

Our oldest daughter and her sister were now on basketball teams, and their brother was playing basketball also. My husband continued the coaching role, which caused a balance in the home. While the change was exciting, it was change nonetheless, not with one person but with five. At the same time, we discovered somethings would have to happen in order for Mary to have her own room. Her siblings were going to make some moves that were going to make them cramped for a while, but everyone was moving together like a well-oiled machine with no squeaks.

All things that settled at our doorstep of change were taken on with prayer and the gatekeeper, my husband. His words were respected as to what was to take place to make this work. I can only imagine how our children got through these times. I know that at this time, there are probably lots of people while reading these lines who are saying, "I was there." With a grateful heart, I say thank you. The prayers were answered with all things working together for good. We called on the Lord in many ways, and He did answer in every way possible. For that I continue to thank the Lord.

Our home was a three bedroom, where the girls shared a room and their brother had his own bedroom. Before the sudden day of change, we were all set for a normal delivery. The crib was to be situated in the bedroom with us, and then as the baby grew older and started to stand up in the crib, it was time for her to move out of our room into one of her siblings' rooms. This was the way we had done it before, so why change, right!

Not so much with Mary. It was almost a forced hand of, "Let's move to make everything work." We thought of our journey as a marathon, not as a sprint we would continue to run as a family. The kids were getting a little tired of fast foods, and we were ready to become a family again. So we set out to do this together, being a little closer than close, but it did come together. We even painted the room periwinkle blue with an excitement of knowing that Mary was coming home soon.

## He's the Man!

I have to stop here and say to my husband, you are so awesome taking on this position of gatekeeper. You were in charge of everything, from the moment of the move from Cleveland to going to the church we were attending right down to having more children, even though I really thought that you were a little crazy. I can now say it was our Father and you were man enough to listen and take control of the gate.

I say to the children today, if their father came into this house with an elephant and said, "We are now going to take on the responsibilities of this animal," I would agree. I must confess I would take him into a personal counseling session, and then we would follow through.

With all that being said, this is the order that comes out of the Word of God that I have chosen to step out on. It's called *submission*, and God has blessed our steps. Even if it would be an elephant, then that means eventually we would own a zoo and there would be an adventure for others to come and see in it the glory of the Lord. The brochure of God's kingdom here on earth as it is in heaven.

I must say with all decisions made, I do have my secret closet that I run to, and I have my real conversations with my Dad with a true, heartfelt purpose, knowing that He always answers me, sometimes with a yes and sometimes with a no or there is no answer at all. In that case, it means I walk out and continue in faith on the last thing He told me. It all began in the pumping room on the sixth floor with a Hallelujah prayer.

**Let's Go!**

With all things set in place, we were now on the space that said, "Go!" The nurse was to be transported to the hospital by the in-home care services, and to be very honest, I do not remember much about how that transfer took place. I can tell you about our wonderful in home care nurses, but on this day my concentration was more focused on everyone being in right position in order for everything to go well for Mary's transfer from hospital to home. I do know that all went well and the nurses were very professional as they saw that I was not walking away when it came to Mary's care. I was very much involved.

It was exciting but at the same time a little stressful. Remember the hospital gowns we used for covering the street clothes and the masking and washing your hands from elbows down? It became a part of the routine in the home. Well, needless to say, I became a little neurotic about these behaviors regardless of who came to visit.

There were many cautions and guard measures given in association with Mary's care, not only with the caregivers but my children and any visitors. They were all given explicit instructions upon entering when planning to visit with Mary. Needless to say, I did tell everyone who called the delicacy of her situation, so the situation with visitors was not that great.

As for the children, they were excited about Mary being home, and they were more than willing, with an understanding of all that we had gone through up until now. We were all in agreement. They would even spy on the nurses and would let me know if they saw anything out of the ordinary, such as the way we would do Meme's hair or the clothing choices made by the nurses, especially if it was a onesie for the day. Mary did receive many outfits as gifts, so they always liked to see her in her outfits during the day, or should I say we. For the most part, the nurses and I would laugh about most of their reports, but everyone knew there were lots of eyes within these Thompson walls.

There was one disease that was mentioned to us called RSV that was the big one so far as the way it was given to us in Mary's exit report. It was the big one to be aware of but not frantic, because the statistics from the hospital showed that the season was passing, and we should be out of the woods.

The signs we were to be aware of consisted of a need for increased amounts of oxygen, increased mucus starting with a form of a cough, and weight gain to extreme amounts (fluids building up). With every shift change, these were small measures to take on with her medication administration, which were given almost on the hour. There were also her feeds that were to be calculated as intake to correlate with the output. She also was having blood work that was taken at the home with a tech who would come out to draw blood. The oxygen tech we met first when he dropped off her in-home tank, which was not to be moved by anyone else except for him, and her portable, which became a good friend of ours, of course with its buddy, her pulse ox meter I can't forget this one with all its bells and whistles. We had a nice little hospital within our home.

## Please Don't Say RSV

We had put a monitor in Mary's room. Even though we had twenty-four-hour nursing care, I still listened in on her care. My rest to say the least was unsettled, especially on the night that I heard the nurse suctioning Mary out. I knew at that point that it was out of the normal pattern of care from the past four or five days. I proceeded to the room diagonally from ours. The nurses, when they were in the room, would turn down the monitor. When I came in, I noticed that she had increased her oxygen, and her sat machine was hovering around a low 80 to 85. The alarm was set to go off below 85.

The nurse reassured me that she would keep an eye on Mary, but she felt pretty confident that it was due to the change from hospital to home and she should bounce right back. Then she smiled and said to me, "Stop looking at the monitors, Mom, and look at your child." Mary was sleeping, so she told me I should do the same, so I did. I thanked her. I was very grateful for these nurses. They were not just nurses; they were moms, aunts, wives, friends, and some were even grandmothers. They were there with us in our home, allowing their gifts and talents to be used in aiding a life that so happened to be our daughter's.

A day or so later, as her health continued to deteriorate, the nurses with their diligence in care for Mary to say the least was amazing. I, on the other hand, started to lose it I felt as though the rug was being pulled from under my feet. I am so glad that my children and my husband were there to give me a separate focus even though it was difficult, more so than when she was at the hospital.

At least at the hospital everything was not seen and getting the report from the night nurse at the hospital is different from standing in your home feeling the pressure. My thoughts were talking loud to my beliefs saying, *Is this it! Are we done just like that! What's the point!*

While I observed the nurses coming out of the normal realm of care, it was so appreciated. We watched Mary go downhill in her health. The close relations with the doctors resumed as the reports were now being given almost on the hour. The doctors were asking for specific nurses by name to speak with to give certain changes in orders.

Eventually the orders were for us to take her to see the pediatrician. This was not the typical first visit after your baby is born. First we walked in with the stroller fully covered with a nurse and our daughter, who also was packing, with oxygen on the side. They knew we were coming and escorted us directly to the back room, which also looked like the doctor's personal office.

The children loved coming here, especially when they were not sick. There was a train that would go through every room. There was a hole cut out in the upper corners of the outer walls, and it was a great distraction. This was our family pediatrician, which was agreed upon before our dismissal. They were also a godsend. You will hear more about them later.

The doctor did a hands-on diagnosis, and from doctor to doctor and pediatrician to hospital, the decision was made that Mary should be admitted immediately. Our instructions were for us to bring her back to UMMS in Baltimore.

We then proceeded to take the nurse home and to drive that well-known ride. They immediately took us in, and her diagnosis came back. They said, "We are sorry to have to tell you this, but Mary's tests have come back positive for the RSV virus." They immediately started prepping her for transfer. I felt the release of the reins again.

One of the emergency room nurses happened to be the nurse who said as we were leaving originally that Mary would be back due to her diagnosis. She approached me as they were taking Mary out of the room to station her on the pediatrics floor and said, "I told you she would be back!" I felt like I was being attacked at all sides, and it was all at the expense of my little Meme.

## We Shall Continue

We were no longer on the NICU floor. We were now on the pediatric ward, which was on the fifth floor. The setup was a little different. As the elevator doors opened, there was a replica of a tree as a waiting play area for the children, with sounds of birds and wildlife as you entered onto the floor.

Mary was set up on the critical side of care, which was

an observation room. Vitals could be seen from a center hub that stationed the doctors and attending nurses. It was structured in a circular, architectural style of hospital rooms and curtain separations in between the rooms. Now we were seeing children, not babies. We did not get a chance to meet any parents on this floor. The transition of healing out of the critical room moved at a lot quicker pace.

There was once a code blue right next door to Meme. There were no blue screens on this floor, so because of the rush, we could see a lot of the interactions of jumping in to save a life. I even saw the paddles go in and the reactions of everyone stepping back and then listening and watching for the signs of life on the monitors. It is so encouraging to see the desperation to save a life, and I thank God for those actions and reactions, especially when the return is life.

Mary remained on this floor until she came home two and a half months later. We received a different doctor, of course, because we were now on the pediatric floor. At first I did not want her to care for Mary. I felt as though since we were in the same hospital that she was just recently released from, it only made sense—to me, of course—that she would just have the same doctors.

Obviously there were still some strong ties that I was not so easily releasing. It took me some time, but I caught on. That doctor ended up being the chosen one for Mary's very difficult transition. All things continued to work together for good!

## Why Am I So Afraid?

At this time, I began to feel quite ill and could not understand what was going on. I would feel feverish and nauseous at times, and then it would go away. I decided that I needed to go see the doctor. At this time my parents also had returned to help us during this transition. They were beyond a blessing in our lives. We were one big, happy family. Even our neighbors were becoming close with my parents and with us as a family.

Well, I went to the doctor, and what he told me was news to me. It really was not expected, and I did not know how to receive the blessed news that we were expecting. It was a little scary, to say at the least. I came home with all kinds of thoughts, and at the top of the list was, *Will this happen again?* The doctor did warn me that it was a strong possibility for me not to go full term, and they would just keep a closer eye on my pregnancy due to the history.

The history was what I was concerned with physically, mentally, and yes, financially. I was actually afraid to face my husband when he came home. As I pulled up to the house, my parents' car was parked in the driveway, so I parked out on the street. When I got out of the van, I saw my neighbor across the street. This was my neighbor who had taken me to the hospital when my water broke. We greeted each other, and all of a sudden I broke down uncontrollably.

At the time she was watering her garden, and she dropped the hose and came running over. She just wrapped her arms around me and asked if Mary was okay. As I settled myself down enough so my speech was cognizant, I expressed to her the report I had just received. I remember her grabbing my shoulders and just looking deep in my eyes with tears welling up in hers. With, that she resumed hugging both of us at the end of our cul-de-sac.

We went into the house, and my mother asked me, "What's wrong, baby?" Just those words coming out of my mother's mouth caused me to start weeping all over again. My neighbor and I ended up sitting on the floor by the couch with some tea my mom had made for us to sip on. As we sipped on our tea, there were not many words exchanged.

The one question that was raised was did Morris know or

had I talked with him, and the answer was no. I really did not know how my husband was going to handle this one, and it was scary. Were we going to continue to carry this one out, or were we going to go to that old route, which was to secretly go and take care of it (abort the child)?

Little did I know at this very same time my neighbor was expecting also! There was one who did know, and He set us up together for such a time as this. She was about to be blessed also with a life to be held and nurtured.

When my husband finally came home, it was an intense moment. First the children came home from school and that was fine going over their individual homework assignments and the activities of the day that they wanted to share with me. I enjoyed this as a distraction to what was currently looming in the back of my mind. Finally I heard the front door open and my husband's normal way of coming into the house is hello in general as the children went running to the door to greet him and he followed through with hugs and kisses. He then looked up and said, "Hey, hon, what's wrong?" As you can tell from his question, my face was still carrying the evidence of lots of tears that was totally missed by the children.

At this point Mom ushered the children out of the room into the kitchen for some sort of snack. I then told him with great hesitation about the pregnancy, and he looked at me and said what I was not expecting at all. He said "So, this is good, and why are you so upset?" I was in a type of shock, and at the same time I was looking at a very changed man. I fell into his arms and just expressed how much I loved him at that point, which was above and beyond what my words could express on paper. I told him I just didn't know how he would react. He then answered with, "How else would I react? This is our child, and we will just love them," with his hand on my stomach.

I also understand why my father admired my husband

so much and how he would always make mention of that to him. What my father saw was a stand-up man, not only for his wife and family but especially for his faith and belief in God.

## Surrogate to Mom

While Mary was in the hospital, we would receive visitors from the sixth-floor NICU, which was comforting and encouraging toward our new relationships we were currently being engrafted into. We did continue to get familiar faces of love and care from the respiratory therapists, which were greatly appreciated.

One therapist was awesome. Our relationship really congealed. She was the one who made the suggestion for Mary's care to include the tape recording in her isolette. She would greet Mary with a, "What's up, Meme girl!" I absolutely loved her approach with confidence in the relationship that she carried with Mary.

There was only one major event while we were on the fifth floor. I believe that this period was another very difficult time because of our bond with Mary transferring home went from a table talk relationship to being handled and fed. Actually, we began to have a mother-daughter relationship.

To be very honest, in a way I held back on releasing myself as a mom. To explain this in words that can be understood, earlier in our relationship I was more of a surrogate mom, standing in a distant position, with faith being my stabilizer. My fear of dropping that role and totally surrendering to being a mom would put me in a vulnerable position. It was a position of surrendering totally to the unknown loving arms of my Father. At this time our relationship was beginning to grow and blossom for others to see.

## Home Again!

We were in the hospital for approximately three months, and I was growing physically with my pregnancy. While visiting one day standing by Mary's bed at a time when we were still not totally out of the woods, a nurse came up to me, put her arm around me, and stated, "God knows all situations, and that's the reason He is giving you a healthy one." I found myself standing there not really knowing how to respond except to say, "Thank you, I guess?" I have found that sometimes when we really don't know what to say, it's okay to say nothing at all, and I am learning this for myself.

During this time of discharge, it was a much more relaxed atmosphere. Mary was growing, her eyes were so much brighter, and her weight gain brought on more activity and a healthier appetite. She had a reflux issue, which means that she tended to upchuck unannounced, which caused added medications to her long list of care. We did have nurses for twenty-four hours for about six months, and then we tapered down to sixteen hours.

## My Expectations in Man

Before we had tapered down, we had an issue with our in-home nursing care. My mom was still there, and this was approximately three to four weeks into our home-care schedule. The shift change was at midnight. Please remember, I was going into my fifth month of pregnancy, and it had been a long day outside of Mary's care. As I checked the time, I noticed that the nurse who came at six o'clock was still there, and it was now about 12:15 a.m.

I went to check in with the nurse to see how everything was going and questioning how they handled a situation when a nurse was running late and what procedures they were to follow. She explained the protocol that was to be followed, and that is what she had done, which was to call the switch board to let them know. Now she would instruct me on what to hand to the nurse when she came to familiarize herself to the case and everything should be okay.

With that her shift was over, and she quaintly said, "Good night," with a reassurance that everything would be okay. She left me with the numbers that were all there in the open on the wall, with all of Mary's medications listed with times of administration.

Mary's meds were not as extreme during the evening hours as they were during the day. Without notice, I found myself in position of caring for my daughter. My initial emotion was intense. I made several calls to find out from the switchboard what exactly had happened and how they were going to get someone out to care for my daughter, understanding the degree of her care and why they did not have a better backup plan. They continued to call back to see if the nurse who was scheduled had arrived. The final call came with, "I'm sorry, Mrs. Thompson, your night nurse will not be coming out, but the nurse for the morning shift has agreed to come in a little earlier."

At this point I was a little distraught about the whole situation, and my mom came in while I was taking in and processing all that was quickly becoming plan B. She continued to rock in the rocking chair with bags under her eyes, with a look of great concern with every phone call.

After the final call, I looked at my mom, and she said, "Denise, we can do this. You just lay down on the floor and I'll watch Meme, and then we can switch after a couple of hours." I didn't want to wake up my husband or the children with any loud noises or sounds that would cause a distress in the home, so I agreed.

After I laid there for about an hour, the Lord touched my

mind with His thoughts, and they were these words of love: "Where are your expectations? Are they in man or are they in Me?" I said to my mom with tears in my eyes, "Mom, my expectations are more in man than in God. I believe He has given us all that we need." My mom agreed, and we hugged. Then I told her to just rest and God would supply. Mom rested in the rocking chair, and I rested on the floor.

I administered all of Mary's meds. My training from the doctor's office started to kick in, and I started to move with confidence. The next morning I set everything up for the morning nurse, who came in a little early. I met her at the door with a hug of gratitude, and I began to give her the night's report.

While we were in Mary's room, I asked her how her family was doing, and I also apologized to her personally and to all the rest of the nurses who had ever come to our home.

I appreciated them as not only as nurses but wives, mothers, daughters, sisters, aunties, and grandmothers; they became gifts, not just names filling a space on the schedule. I genuinely appreciated them sharing their gifts and talents there in our home with our daughter. It was no longer an expectation but an appreciation that came through this whole experience. I began to understand that my faith was truly not in man but in the God who created us all.

*Above and Beyond*

*All in the Family*

*Howard and Clementine Beamer*

*James and Mary Thompson*

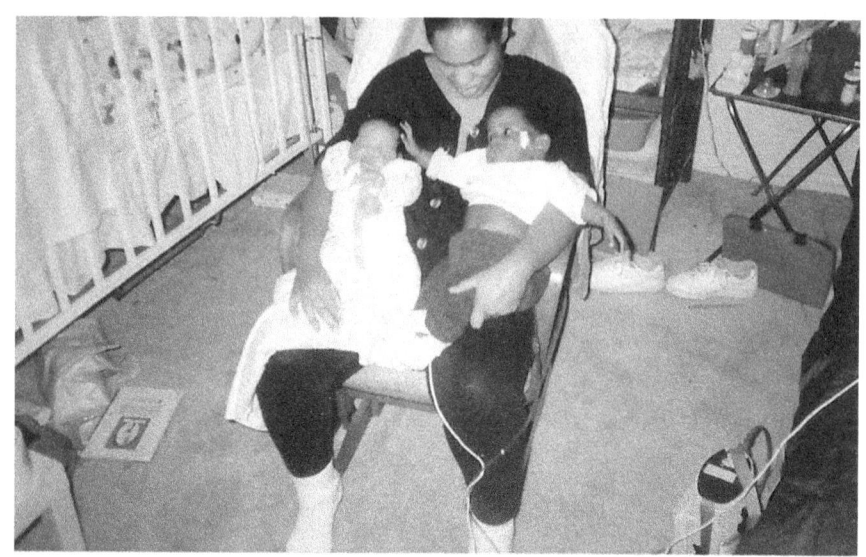

*Lillian with Mary Elizabeth and James Howard*

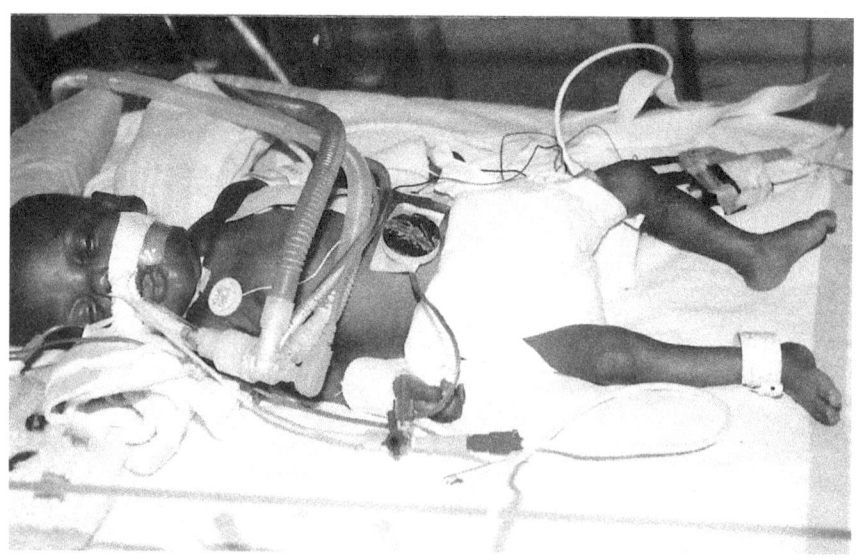

*Mary after being readmitted at UMMS*

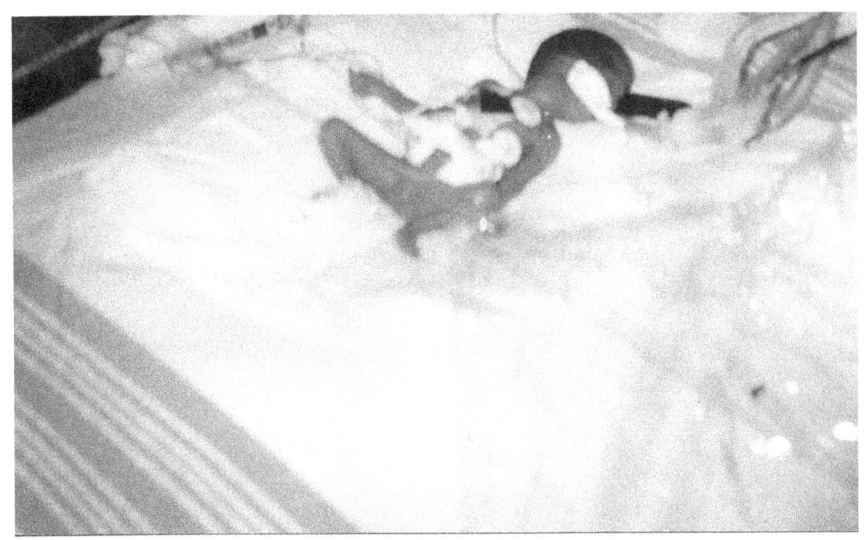

*Mary at 480 grams*

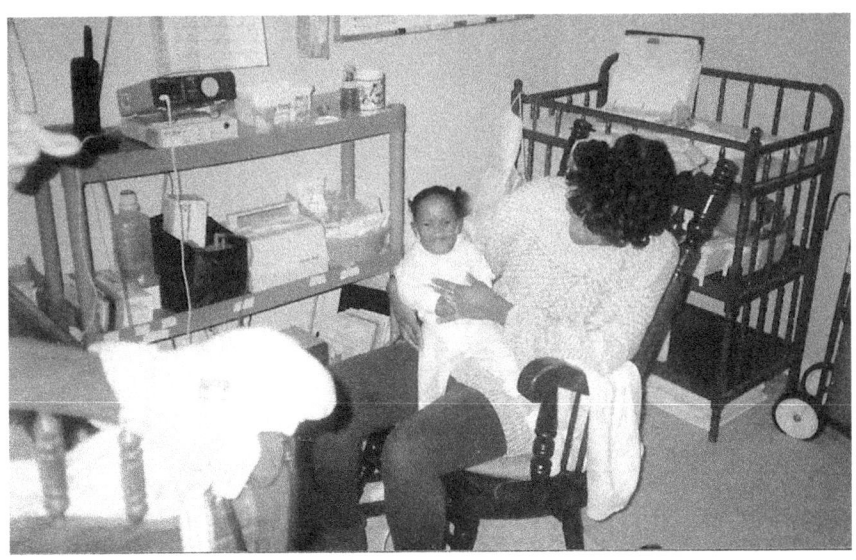

*Mary with one of the in home nurses*

*Morris and Lillian Thompson*

Chapter 8

# School?

O ur *nursing care continued for* about one full year. They became a part of our family. They were there as I continued to grow in stature. Actually our son was growing in leaps and bounds within me. He was born in October of 1993.

He not only went full term, he was also our biggest baby in weight, weighing in at nine pounds, fifteen ounces. He was also our first C-section, which was a great tear jerker to have to change my mind-set from thinking from a normal vaginal delivery to a surgical procedure.

Our family continues to grow, with many blessings in store. All things continue to work together for good, even though in times of troubles it seems like these things in no way could work together for good. The major surgeries continue, not only on me physically with the births of our children but mentally with various ways of healing, which still continues. All I can say at this point is watch me walk. My teacher in life is God. My supplies consist of first and most importantly His Word, which is the author and finisher of my faith. Without His instructions, there would be no explanation to the story that will unfold before your eyes to behold. Come and have a seat as my visitor for the day. Thanks for joining me. Now let's go to school.

As we continued to get back in a normal pace of life outside of the dictates of a hospital being in our lives on a daily basis, we found ourselves preparing for another unknown individual who was continuing to grow and become quite active.

We did not want to do an amniocentesis to discover if there were any abnormalities, which to us made no change in our decisions on having our child. We continued to walk in a way of believing that the one who loved us would continue to give us everything we needed. We did not design them the way they were, but God did. In His Word it states that before we were all in our mothers' wombs, we were in the hands of God.

However, I did have a scare early in this pregnancy where I thought that I had lost our baby with an episode of bleeding. We found out later was that there was a great possibility that I was carrying twins and one did not survive. There was a period of mourning and caution due to the episode occurring so early on in the pregnancy.

## What a Birthday

I know this is starting to sound a bit redundant, but you are probably just going to shake your head on this one. I do understand, and it's a good part of the continuation even though the reoccurrence does continue with a great measure of love inserted each and every time.

At the time of our son's birth, you all know who came down without any hesitancy, and they were—drum roll please—yes! My parents bless, their hearts. They could have entered two zip codes by this time. Also remember we were not their only children in the area My oldest brother and his wife and their children and my oldest sister and her husband lived in the area also, just to broaden your perspective so it doesn't look that mundane. They actually had places to go and escape and enjoy life in other realms of their children's lives as they all were growing flowerbeds of life of their own at the same time.

When I went in to deliver, we were all ready for a normal delivery. It all started with the last visit at the OBGYNs office, with final reports showing signs that more than likely I would be delivering within the next few days on schedule. I find myself having contractions after the visit. We were told that at times the internal exam can agitate the interior to the point that the contractions can be more from a Braxton Hicks type of scenario, but with me being so ripe in the pregnancy, I was told to keep a close record of the pains. If they continued and the time of duration increased and if time span between each one was less than fifteen minutes, we were to call for further instructions.

With that mouthful, over the night the contractions began to increase and shorten, and with that I was told to come to the hospital. Now I must say this was like a vacation compared to my last ride in with sirens and unfamiliar pains. These were familiar pains of a normal birth, and it was a different hospital, which was only approximately twenty minutes away.

The name of the hospital was Holy Cross Hospital in Silver Springs, Maryland. My husband and I came in holding hands. He rolled me in by wheelchair, and they took our names at the emergency room front desk. Then, at a normal pace, they took us to a consultation room to take down all insurance and doctor information, which was common. Then they gave us our bracelets and ushered us upstairs.

With all the pains, I was so enjoying this experience from within. I was praising the Lord continually, with every thank you for all the kind gestures given to pregnant woman coming in to the hospital.

My husband rolled me into our delivery room. This was so cool. There were pretty colors on the walls. It looked like a little hotel room with a hospital bed in the middle of the room. I went to disrobe from my street clothes into my hospital gown in preparation to deliver at full term. This was what was flooding my mind, and also, of course, the pain. I was so thankful between contractions that a couple of times I would shed a few tears.

They started my IV fluids, which I agreed to, and then came the familiar machine of recording contractions. My husband sat by my bedside, with his normal watchful eye on the readout of my contractions, and then he would look at me and ask me, "How did that one feel?" He would congratulate me when he would read the sheet and see the degree of pain that was recorded on the printout.

Now it seemed as though I was plateauing, and no real good reads came as to the cervix opening for a normal process of delivery. It was time to call the doctor to have him come and do an internal diagnosis. My OB was great. He carried the characteristics of a caring father in his bedside manner, which was greatly appreciated. When he came in, he greeted us and collected the readouts and measurements. He then apologized to me for having to do this again but said he would be as gentle and quick as possible.

As he took off his exam gloves after the exam, he told the nurse that her measurements were correct. Then he asked my husband to step out to the hall for a moment. After talking, they came back into the room as he asked everyone to leave for a moment so he could talk with me and my husband.

As my husband draped his arm around my shoulders, the doctor sat on the side of the bed. He held my hand and said, looking directly into my eyes, "Lillian, we are going to have to do an emergency C-section. We do not want to put you or the baby's health in danger, so I have an anesthesiologist waiting, and we are going to do this together, okay?" Immediately I started to cry, and I asked if there was any other way. He looked at me with his fatherly stare, which answered my questions. With that, he gave me a hug of reassurance and encouragement. He also hugged my husband, followed by a handshake of determination between the two.

This was a new experience for me, first of all from my waist down. After curling up like a ball on the table and being as still as I could be regardless of the pain, I received an epidural, which is an experience in itself. I literally could not feel a thing.

A sheet was erected over the top part of my abdomen, and a mirror was added for me to see the delivery. After the incisions were done, I was instructed that I would feel a little pressure, which would be them actually turning my son so they could deliver him. Almost immediately after this occurred, I was told to look. It was a head with pursed lips. He had lots of hair.

At this point, I quickly mentioned to my husband that with all of that hair, that was the reason why I had so much heartburn. He agreed, and we immediately continued to watch this miracle of our son being born.

When he was delivered, I just cried, and of course while watching them clean him up on the table as my husband was admiring his son, I remember the words passing my lips several times over, "Thank You, Father, thank You, Father, You are so awesome!" Then I heard them say, "Wow! "He's nine pounds, fifteen ounces. Mom, get ready, this boy is going to be ready to eat soon." They were oohing and aahing over him as the doctor called out to me, "Lillian, no need for tears now. You did a great job. Look at that beautiful boy!" I got to give him a kiss as I continued to lifelessly lie on the table.

I started to feel a little alone as I lay there and my husband was over there with our son. Every now and then someone would walk over and say, "Great job, Mom!" After all procedures were done, they proceeded to take my son over to the nursery, and my husband followed without hesitancy.

As they continued to suture me up, the doctor explained

the emergency C-section cut that had to be administered and how I was to care for myself after recovery. He did not neglect to let me know that I would be in good hands with the nurses and they would repeat almost everything he had just told me and we should be fine. He then continued to rave about James's weight and health. Thanks, Doc!

## Who's Holding James Now?

Then they took me to recovery, and guess who was there? Without question, it was my mom waiting for me with a big smile. My husband had already given her the news, and she was beaming! She gave me a big hug, and I asked her if she had seen him. She said, "Not yet, but I can't wait to see him. Is it true that he weighs nine pounds, fifteen ounces?" Of course we all know the answer to that question by now.

I heard a cart coming into the recovery room, and the nurse checked my bracelet with his. Then she proceeded to prepare him to be handled, and my mother was helping me to raise up on the bed in a comfortable position. Then my moment finally arrived; I got to hold my son. Then the nurse said something that I was not expecting. She asked my mother if she was grandma, and she answered positively. Then she asked her if she wanted to hold him, and my mother, of course, responded with a resounding, "Oh, yes!" Then she handed my son over to my mom!

That is still a joke we tell on our son's birthday that his mom was not the first to hold him; it was his grandmother—that is, the first other than his dad. When we would remind my mom of that, she would just laugh and say, "Well!" as though it were a well-deserved privilege. In all honesty, it was a nice gesture from Dad, with perfect timing.

My first time admiring this little bundle of peace was so gratifying. As I looked at those big eyes and all that hair, those little fat fingers, and his little feet, they were so cute. I called them Fred Flintstone feet. I loved kissing those fat cheeks. James was so complacent that he didn't cry much, which was such a blessing. Everybody held him with a look of awe, all toward Your ways, Dad. I could never set things up the way You have and continue to do so perfectly.

## God's Timing Is Perfect

A couple of days later, I was becoming more accustomed with a pillow relationship due to the surgery. This is a common comforter among women who have had C-sections. Whenever I would go to move or walk, it was my constant friend. It was so exciting to get my legs back so I could actually get up to walk down the hall and take a peek when I wasn't going to pick him up, just getting my limbs back into working order.

That first night in the hospital my husband stayed all night. Before I could walk well without assistance, he went to take our son back to the nursery, and there was a pleasant surprise. There just happened to be a woman standing on the outside of the nursery waiting to receive her baby, and this woman was my neighbor! She had delivered earlier that day also. Obviously she did not have a C-section!

We had actually delivered almost at the same time with the same OB without even knowing it. How amazing is that! When she came around the corner and said, "Hey sweetie!" I gasped with a flabbergasted look and then tears. She came over to the bed, and we just hugged.

Our words were short and taken by the moment of the shock and wonderful gift of the unexpected, abundant life we were experiencing together as we embraced each other. I got a chance to see her precious gift of life, and she was just beautiful beyond words. While I write these words, all I can continue to say is, "All things work together for good for those who love the Lord."

## What Child Is This?

Becoming a family of extraordinary ways of doing things, we were able to return to church for service. Our pastor had instructed us to advise him whenever we came with Mary because he wanted to pray over her with the deacons of the church, which we promised we would do.

Well, the first time coming back we had our son James, and Mary had to stay at home with the nurse, who actually encouraged us in returning, since Mary's needs were not as great as they were in the beginning. We were comfortable with her being there with no eyes in the house to spy on her. As was mentioned before, we were like family.

While entering the church, we did not make any announcements as to our comings. We actually came in after service had begun and worship service was in progress. We were willing to be seated in the back in case we needed to leave for any reason.

As service progressed and the sermon was given, we prepared ourselves for the benediction and then to leave quietly. I began to give a look over toward the children with a visual type of directing as to our preparing to leave. Lovingly as always, Pastor looked out over the crowd and recognized us in the back of the church. He resounded with an announcement of awareness of some good friends of his that he would like to bring forth.

I was thinking to myself, *Oh no, Pastor, this is not Mary!* At the same time, he was assembling the Deacons in the front for prayer. When my husband and I approached the front of the church with James, I was trying to keep his attention so I could mouth to him while pointing, "Pastor, this is not Mary, this is James." He didn't see it until we came to the front. I whispered in his ear, "Pastor, this is not Mary, this is James." He started to chuckle a little, and he explained that this was not who he thought it was and that we had surprised him with another blessing. With exchanges of slight laughter, he reached out to embrace James.

Pastor's eyes became enlarged as he exclaimed, "Boy, what have you been feeding him?" I just gave him the look of, "Pastor, please, I am embarrassed enough." He then continued to explain the story of Mary and that as a celebration for all in waiting. Such as the case with Pastor, he responded without a stutter that with James, it too would be a day of celebration of life from the hand of God to be recognized.

With all of that being said, he then proceeded to bless James and my husband and me. His prayers were blessings bestowed upon us to continue in the way that the Lord was leading us through His Word with our family. The church unanimously said, "Amen!" It was kind of hilarious, but it was all scheduled by the one who is already in our tomorrows.

## The Blessings of the Lord

Events in our home were becoming more familiar, even with the nurses. There were even a couple of nurses who rededicated their lives to the Lord and one who even accepted the Lord Jesus as her Savior, which was very cool.

Our home was becoming more and more sensitive to these blessings of life coming in all sizes from all places. We came to realize it was not about the dos of the individuals but the whos or the people we were personally becoming familiar with. I found a gift of exhortation (encouraging others) and a building up toward not only the nurses but also their families, our children and their friends and families, family from Cleveland and beyond, our church family and their friends. We were hearing about many transformations in so many individuals' lives as they would just deposit these reports within the walls of our home. It was truly a blessing (Phil. 2:12 AMP; Jer. 33:9).

We even had several occasions when the hospital would call and ask for us to talk with other families as they were coming through similar situations, with the same actions being recognized as a faith base of choice. With some families, the outcome became more extensive. The hospital even requested our presence in a nurses' seminar as a family who was willing to share our rare situation with a willingness to even bless the nurses with a greater understanding toward the emotional side of the patient, and when it comes to faith it is important to be sensitive to a family's stance as not to fear it but to talk with the patients and to continue loving them as they did with us. We expressed our appreciation for their outstanding care while we were patients within the walls of UMMS on floor number six.

Our relationship with the hospital was very interesting to say the least. We truly grew together. I have come to some understandings that we are all practicing physicians in different fields of life with varied qualifications that are all being used to build up lives.

## Can We Talk?

My neighbor who is like my sister asked one time with curiosity, "What church do you go to?" I looked at her and said, "I attend a Baptist church, but that isn't it. I really love Jesus because He has loved me like no other!" Well, we both just smiled and said to each other in jest, "That is it!" Nothing else needed to be said except a hug and a giggle like little girls with a great secret to share with each other. It was great and still is. Whenever we talk or see each other, it is a knowing without explanation.

At this point, my children were young. With their disagreements and small fights, as they became accustomed to the nurses they began to portray their real faces without any holding back whatsoever. It was mainly the two middle ones, our son and daughter, who were very competitive. It started to come off the field and come into the house, and it was not pretty. At times, to be very honest, it was downright ugly. I felt very frustrated at times, but I would then have them come to me and we would talk and pray together.

The encounters were difficult initially, but in the end there would be a peace, at least for a little while. As I previously recounted, I remembered the time when I found myself in a peculiar situation with an inward transformation that took place. I was in a store in line with the rest of the parents, and we were preparing to send our children back to school after summer vacation. I found myself not affirming the conversations that were surrounding me. I could not agree with a clear conscience, and it was confusing me. What I was unable to agree with were the expressions of celebration of sending the children back to school.

I felt a surge of wanting to continue especially with our devotions and times of closeness. We had huddle times of immediate regrouping, with the Word of God being the initiator. This was weird to say the least, and I really did not know immediately who to talk to in this awkward mindset. It was so contrary to all the ways I had ever known.

Soon after the back-to-school moment of confusion, I recalled those early days in Cleveland and the peace I felt in the home. Then it came to my attention that our current pastor and his wife also were homeschooling. I proceeded to call First Lady and ask her if I could come over and talk with her about the homeschooling thing. My husband and I had discussed it and decided that it would be a good idea to talk with our pastor and first lady about it and then figure out if this was really something we wanted to do.

Our visitation with Pastor and First Lady and their family was a blessing. Not only was our question on whether we would be homeschooling answered, but a focus from the Lord was acknowledged, and it was not of the world. Our children blended well in age and also in characteristics. They were children! As First Lady and I sat in their kitchen and Pastor and my husband sat in the living room, we talked, laughed, and prayed. We shared real deal issues of the day and the heaviness of a change that came upon us years ago. Now it was back, with a clear path that was so easily being laid out before us by our pastor and his wife. Peace was the governor of their decision to homeschool.

## I Believe We Are Ready!

At one point while First lady and I were talking, we heard a noise under the table. It was my son attempting to sneak away while we were talking. At this point we looked at each other, smiled, and continued talking while pretending as if we did not see him. Then one of the other children came in ever so slyly so we would not see them. At this point, we let them know we had detected their game and they would have to think of a new game that did not involve us or Pastor and Dad.

With a little probing, we discovered what game they were playing. It was called "The Reporter." They had been taking notes from our conversation and trying to put it all together with the bits and pieces they were acquiring from each other. They were actually taking pretty detailed notes. We were surprised and also thankful that our conversations were not concerning other issues.

First Lady also showed me some of the curriculum she had used and described to me how the lessons were laid out. Then all of a sudden she started piling all these books on me, and as she put it, "That should be a good start for you!" I just stood there in a sort of stupor of thanksgiving. It was awesome, and I felt so ready to start homeschool!

**Medicines, Nurses, Faith**

With this moment of awakening, there were other items on the table of life that needed some rearranging. The nursing care in our home, instead of a stabilizer, was now becoming a weight with straps that we needed to remove in love. The nurses were now becoming extensions of our family; however, we could sense that their care would be coming to an end as Mary's meds and care began to be cut back, which also came miraculously.

On the one Sunday we were able to take Mary to service, it was so peaceful. Of course we had planned it out with the pastor and arranged to have a specific nurse to attend with us on this particular day. When they prayed over Mary as they had done with James, the difference, of course, was in line with her condition. She still had a need for oxygen and several meds, and of course the most evident was the nursing care.

All of these things were prayed over that they would no longer be a part of our lives. As we continued, within a few weeks her meds started dropping off. After subtle questioning, we found that she was showing definite signs of no longer having a need for these meds. At this point, the need was not as great for certain medications. They were decreased, and some were just stopped immediately.

Her oxygen was one of the last prescribed meds to go. We said good-bye to the oxygen tank, and not shortly after that came our severing ties with the nursing care, which was a very scary moment, I cannot lie!

The scary moment of the tapering down of the nursing care happened after a medical scare with a chicken pox breakout, which was literally diagnosed on the day the last nurse was packing up to leave our house.

Our daughter had a classmate who was highly contagious in school. He was not aware of what the illness was or that it was contagious. The weekend before the breakout in our house and the ending of the nurses, my mom and I at times on Saturdays would go out to neighborhood garage sales. While at one of our neighbors' tables, the mom was expressing to those who were closer in relation to her situation that they would need prayer because their son was getting worse and was currently hospitalized.

Of course my ears perked once I heard of a situation with a child being under some type of medical attack, so I inquired. When she expressed to me her son's situation, almost immediately we started to recognize each other as I shared my story of our daughter's hospitalization and extensive care. Her eyes became wide, and she exclaimed to me that my daughter and her son were in the same class, which was wonderful, and at the same time it drew my attention to some areas of my home. Now I was on the prayer path of rebuking this disease that could set us back again into the hospital, especially with Mary.

The pediatrician had forewarned us that the chicken pox disease could set Mary back, especially because of her susceptibility to lung disease. We continued on our path, still walking out our beliefs and praying like there was no tomorrow as we embarked upon the final day of sign off and reports from the nurses.

While all of this was on the table, our concentration was on our daughter's physical activities, especially at school. She had to feel a little out of sorts because of the constant questionings from me and the nurses concerning the symptoms. We were continuing to look out for signs like fever or raised bumps in the form of a triangle, which were concrete signs of chicken pox.

The final nurse, who had become a close friend at this time, as she was preparing to leave, I continued to stress to her my belief that God was going to continue to take care of us no matter what. I was actually convincing myself to continue to stand in my faith. Of course, one of the main questions was directed to our daughter showing any signs of chicken pox. My answer was a negative. I asked her off the clock as a friend if she could look at a couple of bumps I had just detected on her back, which also was one of the things to look out for. The nurse took a look at my daughter's back with her concerned way of observing, and with a deep breath, she said, "It looks like chicken pox."

She then emphasized that it was not mandatory that nursing should end at this time, since I was the one who was requesting that nursing be stopped. It was very hard, but it was a strong step for me to make by faith instead of holding onto those straps of support from the nurses. I needed to truly trust in the Lord in this outbreak of chicken pox and believe He was not going to leave us in this situation either. We prayed together, and in turn we said our good-byes.

There was a terrible breakout in our house of chicken pox. Our daughter ended up being quarantined from the others, which hurt my heart because I was the only one who had contact with her. She did not end up in the hospital, but she did have a bad breakout. Mary did contract the disease, but before it occurred, because I knew there was a high probability that she could contract the disease, I had her inoculated and her baby brother also. They both contracted the disease, and both cases ended up being minor. God was faithful. We came through the fire. It was like a course of standing in the storms without our extra external supports but standing as a family of faith in love, and we made it! Glory be to God. In all seriousness, that was a real step of faith in the school of love.

## A New Normal

My parents returned home, and we became a normal family and now did things together as a family. We packed up the car when leaving the house with five children and one on the way. That's right, number six was now on his way into the "Three is enough for me" family to make it more of the supernormal that we knew not of. But remember we are in school, and there are lessons to be learned along the way.

With number six, there were not as many anxieties, and actually we were even going to try to have a normal vaginal delivery, which was a possibility. With my visits to the pediatrics office, we ended up with some of Mary's original caretakers from UMMS, who were residents and doctors on staff at the time. It was as if all things continued to be set up for us to continue on this path that was not heavily traveled. I was continuing to see the hand of God, which for me was amazing. I started to truly believe in the Scripture that says, "Trust in the Lord with all your heart and lean not on your own understandings and He shall direct your path" (Prov. 3:5).

## Isaac or Issac?

My obstetricians continued to be the best that God called them to be at the time. Our son was born at term, and we did end up having a C-section because he decided at the time of delivery to turn. We had to do an emergency ultrasound and found out that our son was breech. Our son came out laughing. Let me clarify. When they brought him to me and I held him for the first time and I said hello to this beautiful blessing from God, he looked at me and smiled and laughed!

He has been making us laugh ever since. We named him Michael Issac. His middle name came out of the Bible which means laughter.

What is still funny for us today is that while in school, there is the spelling part. As I initially typed out his name, it got red lined, and yes, it is incorrectly spelled. We didn't realize that until later because of a crossword puzzle that all the letters were not matching up until we looked up the correct answers. We had to laugh again because of the correct spelling of Isaac. Just make a little cheat sheet in case you run into similar situations in naming your child or doing a crossword puzzle.

## A Toenail?

Our church family at this time was continuously growing by leaps and bounds to the point that it was almost unrecognizable to us. At the time of Mary's delivery, our church moved to a new location. The congregation continued to grow, with the Word of God being the initiator of the growth of sheep making sheep. At one point in time, I ended up writing the pastor a letter, letting him know that I was still there in the body but not as noticeable. I considered my position to be more of the toenail of the body, piggybacking on his message that touched my heart, which led me to write the letter.

His message came out of having a hurt toe or toenail and how it affected his whole body. I saw my position as not being played out in the church but more so out in the world. Even though I considered myself to be a toenail, I knew we were still all one body. With that being said, my prayers were arranged in order for the body to be aware of our importance to our Father within the body for such a time as this. We must not allow our feelings to dictate our importance but continue in the body of Christ believing the Word of God as being the author of our positions in life in love.

## It's a New Day

Going on our outings to the soccer games was great. I had the same big bag that I carried Mary's books in to the hospital, but now it served a new purpose. Not only did it carry books but toys—toys from McDonalds and other fast food places we had been collecting from those former years of no consistency of home-cooked meals.

I remember *Toy Story* was big then, and we had collected every talking Woody and Buzz Lightyear out on the fast food toy market. All the smaller children loved coming over to our blanket. The snack time allowed me to bring out the graham crackers and water. With all of these festivities on the blanket, at the same time I was preparing for homeschooling off the blanket.

We had successfully gone through the process of buying our home and had started looking around at new building sites because it looked as though my husband was about to take on another job that would put us in a better position to quite possibly buy a new home. This was all so exciting. The house was very comfy and we loved it, but it was exciting to have a hope of buying a home where the children could have more space to live in and we could continue to grow as a family. At the same time, my prayers were being guided in a way to bless another family. I felt so strongly about this that even as I would clean the house, it was as if I could see them being blessed with this home. It didn't exactly work out that way, but my heart was directed in this way to think of others and not of self during this time.

The other item that was being magnified in the process of my thinking was to take care of the little and in that more would come. I did not feel strapped to either end of the living experience but enjoyed the travels through the seasons of life as they came, believing that all things were possible and enjoying it all.

## New Job, New Responsibilities

My husband did get the new job, but I remember him saying to me as we prayed about it that he would not be at home as much because that his time would be consumed more at work. With more pay came more responsibilities. I heard him but I didn't. I was so excited about the new homes that we were pursuing that it was the least of my worries.

## Laying the Groundwork for Homeschool

Homeschooling began with an understanding of school and teaching that I was raised with, which was just taking public school and bringing it into my home. I did not do it intentionally, but it was the only concrete foundation I could see to stand on at the time. It consisted of early morning breakfast with classical music playing in the background because I was told this would bring right thoughts in order for learning. We then would of course have our devotional time, which was truly a blessing. We would start with praise and worship songs, and then there was prayer, taking on the patterns that had been well impressed into my being. Then there was Scripture basketball. For every Scripture they had memorized, they were given an opportunity to shoot a ball of socks into a basket, and if they made the shot, they received a gift or a chore removal. Then there was a short story from the Bible, which ended our devotion time.

Now it was time for real school. We put down the Bible and picked up the books that I could truly teach from. What I did not realize was that I was teaching my children the same standards that I used to question, because they did not match up with the Bible stories. I was safe, and my children were very compliant, especially since they had recently been excused from the walls of public school. Our favorite outing was to the library to get books, VHS tapes, books on tape, and tapes with children's instructional sing-alongs.

Another favorite of ours that still continues is what we call opposite world. Opposite world thinking came out of a class I had been taking for weight loss at our church that was teaching me a different approach to losing weight. It involved a change of thinking. It changed the way I thought not only with weight loss but my life choices altogether. I ended up losing at least fifty pounds. I aligned my thoughts with the Word of God and followed through in life trusting in His Words more than man's.

It was a time of trusting in the Word of God and no longer leaning on the traditional ways of thinking that I was slowly becoming aware of. Understanding that, the way we were choosing to teach also was slowly changing into an opposite world way of thinking. We were finding out that this way was the freeway of life with no tolls to pay.

One of our first on purpose not-of-this-world trips was to Disney World. It was at the beginning of September, and the park was free from crowds and multiple lines. What we have found is that when we go on trips or simple outings, we find peace. We find ourselves at parks with no lines, empty movie theatres, empty restaurants, and empty stores with time available to speak with actual courtesy and have real conversations with people who are working or are out at the same time. My husband will even schedule his time when available to meet us, and we have a ball. Before a movie, we will complain about those people who are talking too, loud and we ask them to keep it down; we are actually talking to each other. These are some of the fun days of our homeschool that can never be replaced.

## Speak to My Heart, Lord
We also gathered with other families in the church who

were homeschooling. It was a small number, but it was a true blessing. We really felt like a family. Then as the church grew, so did the homeschool groups. We were still associated with the sports activities in the community, which also had started to grow as our community started to grow in leaps and bounds. There was a major growth spurt going on in the area, which was truly a blessing, but at the same time we found ourselves a little disheveled by the growth pains of church and community. It became a pick-and-choose time of life as to what was best for the family.

With our permission, Chiara started attending another church that had programs that her gifts were being used in. We attended a few times, and it was a Word church. What I mean is that the Word of God was leading the pastor and not the world. I still had my ties with our other church, so it continued to be a visitation, which meant parking in the visitor's spot with confidence.

Our visitations became more frequent, and it also incorporated our recent move into our new home. We were not only moving in a physical way but also in a mental and spiritual way. I decided to schedule a time of consultation with the pastor of the new church we were attending because my visitations had become more regular. Out of respect for my name not being currently on the roll, I did want to bring to his attention that this would only be for a short period of time because I was not a member. I proudly told him that I was a member of another church. He acknowledged it with grace and let me know that he knew my pastor and thought he was a great pastor. In turn I agreed. He also threw me a curveball. Well, not really—it was a straight shooter. He said that he felt I should talk with my pastor concerning my attendance and incorporation with his church and number one to pray and ask the Father and to follow through from there.

I took his advice and went into prayer concerning a conversation with my pastor. I gave him a call, and we got a chance to discuss the trivial matter of my attendance and why we had found ourselves now attending the other church. I asked what his views were on the situation. In my mind, as I am talking with Pastor, I felt as though he would want me to figure out how we could return and reincorporate ourselves back into the fold. Not exactly; what Pastor had to say humbled me. He stated clearly that he felt it would be best if we continued at the new church with his blessings.

To this day, our pastor says that he does not remember ever saying that to me, but I believe it was the Holy Spirit that was speaking because of what happened next. At first, to be honest, I felt offended, but I took my offense to prayer and continued my course. In my prayer, I asked the Lord to make it clear to me as to whether I should join the new church or reintegrate with our old church.

That very next Sunday, I parked for the very last time in the visitor's parking space. The parking lot had stones as a surface, so as I was walking—I remember this so clearly—I started shuffling my feet and kicking the stones, dreading the fact that at this church the people didn't know me. They didn't have the serious praise and worship I was so used to at my old church. At this point I was thinking, *I already know the answer, so let me get over this one and chalk it up to experience. Thanks, Dad!*

I entered the sanctuary during their praise and worship time. This was a more conservative type of church, not as up tempo, but the one thing that was strong within their walls was their children's ministry and youth ministry. They were truly on fire for the Lord, which was exciting. As I entered one of the back pews, I heard a voice say, "Is this all about you?" It was actually my inside voice, and as it struck, I became convicted.

The other thing about this church was it was not as vocal as my other church. Remember how I talked about the conversing from the pulpit to the congregation? Well, not so much with this church. Even with that being a difference, there was one huge detail that was very much the same, and that was the Word of God. It continued to speak to me the same way regardless of the form or fashion of the congregation. I found myself still having conversations with the pastor of this church as if we were the only ones in the sanctuary, because as he spoke he was speaking directly to my situation, and I was willing to respond.

It was kind of funny when I was not at church on Sunday for whatever reason. One of the members would come up to me and say, "We missed you last Sunday. Is everything going all right?" It was cool.

On this particular Sunday, there was now conviction, and I was looking for an answer to my question concerning joining this church. As I observed the pulpit, the pastor was not there. It was a visiting Pastor. This was just getting better, or so I thought. As we moved into the end of the message, I noticed that he didn't do the altar call or make mention of those the Lord had moved on their hearts to join this particular congregation as a part of the family. No, but he did say, "There is someone who is questioning why they are here. Let me tell you it is not about you, it is all about Him, Jesus, so come and allow Him to use you today."

I had to sit down, and at the same time I started to cry because He could not have made it clearer for me. I got up and went to the front of the church in repentance (a changed mind).

It was not about me; this was all about my Father. I was crying so profusely that one of the deaconesses said in my ear while handing me a tissue, "It is wonderful when you accept the Lord Jesus Christ in your life." I tried to tell her but it just wasn't coming out clear, so I gave up even trying. It was okay;

at least God my Father knew where my heart was at this time, and that was all that mattered.

## The School of Life

As we were continuing our homeschool, I found myself integrating with various groups of people depending on the activity or function our children were branching off into depending on their passions as some were dying out and others were sparking.

We found ourselves befriending a homeschool family. We saw that they had similar characteristics. They had eight children who were in the same age range as ours. The mom had a degree in the area of special education, which made it refreshing to have someone to talk to in that realm every now and then. They lived in the next neighborhood over, which made it even better.

Mary's care had transitioned from in-home care to in-home schooling through a public school service that was extended to us because of her new classifications of learning. Even before the nurses had left, the physical and occupational therapists were coming out to put her on course in her development, not only physically but also mentally. This was a transitional situation that was preparing us for Mary's care to go from in the home to going into a public school that was a separate institution of learning on a hill up in the woods.

It was a beautiful building inside and out; it was what was inside that made this facility truly beautiful. It was the people who took on these teaching responsibilities, which in many cases were extreme mental disabilities. I found myself in a new world that I knew not of. I struggled with this plan due to the fact that I had just recently started to homeschool all of Mary's other siblings.

So we went from going to the bus stop to a little yellow

school bus coming to our house and picking up our one child. That caused us to stop in our tracks of the so-called traditional ways of not only schooling but transferring over into the mindset of opposite world. This was a difficult situation for me mentally, and I just could not wrap my mind around this one.

What was starting to become a realization for me was a factual assessment. Walking by faith and not by sight was becoming a mainstay in the school of life. At times I felt as though I understood the teacher's ways of teaching, so at times I would go on my own assumptions as to how to handle certain items, believing them to be trivial to even bring to the teacher's attention. In my mindset, I already knew how it was to be assessed from past situations of learning.

What I am finding out is that I have to return to class and stop skipping class because I already understand the syllabus and the teaching style. I took my notes, and I even have recordings of the teacher's lessons. It pays to return to class in the morning and allow the teacher who actually knows us better than we know ourselves to teach us. His teachings are always in a right order for such a time as this. Day by day His Word has never failed me but only encouraged me to step out of the box and become more of a reflection of His love here on earth as it is in heaven.

Chapter 9

# My Sarah Moment

I *find myself looking over the* many diverse turns in the direction of my life. It has been and continues to be a journey of true living, and I must say that I am enjoying the ride. There are moments that take me truly to places I personally would not even imagine. Such is the case with our suddenly move to a place that never entered my mindset as a place of dwelling. I had imagined San Antonio, Texas, as I would continue to brush up on my Spanish as a second language (which I am still pursuing). For a short period of time, we even thought about moving back to Cleveland. It was a fleeting moment. We at one time even thought of moving to Spain. This too was a fleeting thought.

Where we ended up was a place called Virginia; yes, the state of Virginia. The place of the first successful English settlement was here. We know it today as the good old United States of America. I have found myself in the woods of Pocahontas State Park and literally could visualize the Native Americans and their thoughts as they were living their lives in a manner of order that was in the Algonquin tribal way. In the summer, there was no need for shoes, or should I say moccasins, and vice versa in the winter months, which in general are pretty calm. They had a way of life that was conducive for survival within the land they were living in and actually thriving.

These accounts of life became more traditionally known through oral accounts that were written down by the English as they explored the new people groups and territory.

Now it was my turn. The year was 2001, and we said, "Happy New Year!" in prayer and excitement, for there were now nine of us, and life was good for the most part. Let us partake of the travels in a new land together. I will unfold some of my written accounts as they were already etched out in His Word, taking on characteristics of an on-purpose life. Finally, stepping out and believing His word, to be the author and the finisher of my faith by standing out like the three Hebrew boys.

## From Pit to Paradise

We made it through the year 2000, which was a year of jubilation to say the least. Our seventh blessing of completion had been delivered unto us in the miraculous form of a little girl. Her birth was miraculous to us personally due to the fact that in 1998 I was expecting in the early summer months. I was very active with the children; we were so excited in our new home. There was a lot of hands-on decorating. I took on the learned talents from my walking buddy of sewing, and I took several sheets and made curtains for all the rooms. I also furnished the majority of our home with thrift store furniture, which was fun as I found those items like coffee tables, accent tables, lamps, and of course the occasional clothing shopping details. I believe it was on Tuesdays that they would tag certain sections of the thrift shop as half off, and I was right there knowing which items I wanted to purchase for our home that week or within that month.

Our oldest daughter started working at Sears, so I knew when all of the good sales were on, especially in the home decorating department. I would get used cans of paint that had been returned and wallpaper remnants that had been discontinued. Finding all of the treasures was exciting to say the least. I took on my mother's love for working in the garden and taking care of the lawn. Since we were living in a new development, we also found unwanted building materials that the builders let us know were all good for the taking.

With the building materials, I got the grand idea that we would build a tree house, so we went to our favorite spot—the library—and researched building a tree house. We researched everything, right down to picking the appropriate tree that had good structure to build a tree house in. It had a strong Y base, which was essential.

While acquiring these materials from a heap out on an open lot, there was a large sheet of plywood that we found that was perfect for the flooring of our tree house. As my son and daughter were trailing me holding the opposite side of the plywood, I stepped back into a hole and found myself in sudden darkness.

After being knocked out for some time and then looking up into a blue sky with two faces of worry looking on, I gingerly got up with a slight pain in my back and within my abdomen. I played it off well enough to continue carrying the wood to the spot and proceed into the house. I then rushed to the bathroom because I felt a sensation of slight moisture between my legs. I was praying that it was just sweat. Unfortunately it wasn't; it was blood. What I was experiencing was a miscarriage.

I called the doctor's office, and when they heard the details of what had just occurred, they confirmed my assumptions. It was followed up with an appointment that gave us the final report of terminated pregnancy. I had a surgical procedure called a D and C, which for me felt similar to an abortion. The sounds and the smells took me mentally to a bad space, and of course I couldn't tell the attending physician what was going on in my head. I put on the face and played the role with tears that were genuine from a hurting heart.

I felt as though it was no longer in the cards for me to have any more children. I could not go through this again. It was mentally and physically to difficult for me to even think in this arena anymore. I just felt like giving up.

After all of this, I leaned on my dear friend who, through a miraculous stripping of self between the two of us spiritually, became my prayer partner. We prayed with and for each other continuously. At this time we were expecting together, so our prayer partnership was a joyful time until the fall. I felt as though mentally I was in a pit, and it was difficult to say kind words concerning her pregnancy since I was no longer traveling the same happy, happy, joy, joy road. We had encouraged each other prophetically also that we were claiming girls. We continued to pray together, and it became no longer me but the Word of God that truly led my words, and my actions would slowly follow. That next spring my prayer partner gave birth to a beautiful baby girl, and when I went to see her at the hospital, I was genuinely excited about what God had done with our lives. We were finding ourselves giving up on self-efforts and looking toward the one who truly loved us.

Nine months later, I did have number seven, and she was and is a beautiful girl who was born full term with no problems or issues. The pediatrician who was doing rounds at the hospital on the day of her release was my old doctor friend. With great joy, he checked her out, and the look that we gave each other with an inward knowing as to how this began. With hugs and congratulations, he released her from the hospital. We named her Amaris, which means promised by God.

While carrying my promise from God, I did have a God moment that hit me later in life. I will share it with you. As I had mentioned, I felt unsure whether I was to have any more children, and I had many naysayers in the camp, me included. One day my husband and I, with all the children, were visiting my brother and his family up in Hinkletown, Pennsylvania. Yes, it is a small town. There was a average-size farmhouse that sat off the side of the road with a semi-circular driveway and a few trees lining the drive with a grassy center where you would normally on a sunny day see children playing and adults standing around or sitting in lawn chairs. There were constant, visible signs of life that surrounded this residence on Route 322. It was like the heart pulsating in the center of town.

On this particular day, I remember opening the storm door, walking into an open country kitchen, and seeing a sweet, graceful elderly woman sitting at the kitchen table with her sister at her side. Her eyes were looking on the entryway, and without words, I felt and received a warm welcome. She called out my name and told me to come, and without question I did. I gave her a gentle hug and did the same with her sister. I sat down, and she reached over and held my hand with slight releases, with a pat here and there.

She asked me how I was doing, and I told her the obvious, which was that I was pregnant and not feeling very accepted by the crowds that were currently surrounding me and my family. She then grabbed my hand with a squeeze and told me that I was blessed with a blessing from the Lord and to consider myself to be a blessed child of God. She also told me to not let the world dictate who I was but God. She reassured me to continue being a good mom and wife.

I felt like a used car that was sitting on the used car lot with signs of abuse. I had been stolen several times and stripped and taken out for numerous joyrides by anyone and everyone. And then the original owner walked up on me and said, "Here she is!" I was feeling a little confused. "Are you talking about me? Have you taken a good look at the body? And what about my mileage? It's way up there!" He sat in me and said, "She is perfect now that she is back in my hands." He said, "Relax, I've got you. All the old scars are repairable, and I have erased those old miles. You can run the way you were designed to if you only allow me to sit in the driver's seat so I can steer you in the right direction." He installed a GPS that I could read, and every now and then, with a still, soft voice, it gave me directions when needed for all the right turns. I gave up the wheel once again, and He smiled and revved me up. Then it was time to fill up with the fuel that is needed to continue.

Here I was looking into the eyes of a godly woman who had lived most of her life, and with some of what was left, she was extending herself in love to me. She was not only a sister, but she was a wife to one man for several decades, a mother of seven girls, a grandmother to at least twenty-seven, and a great-grandmother to at least fifty. This woman had lived and was living what she was telling me to do with a look that was so piercing to my soul. This caused a change in my thinking.

She left this earth two years later. She never got a chance to see Amaris, but if it were not for her words and her life, which I saw being lived before me, it would've been hard for me to hold my head high in love. When she passed, all of her children were there and her husband. She left her legacy in peace, knowing that with her life she continued to stand on a truth that did not change and her children can always remember, if nothing else, that Mom, Grandma, Great-Grandma, Great-Great-Grandma stood on the Word of God. That is the truth I want to leave my children, grandchildren, great-grandchildren, and all those generations to come.

## Seven Brings Completion

Wow! Seven was a completion in more ways than one. As I found myself continuing down this road of life, it became an adventure of seeking a new route. This is the day that the Lord has made, and I shall rejoice in it. I now look forward with confidence, knowing that God has already been in this day. I am going to take the time out to acknowledge Him with a course that has already been arranged for me by Him if I am willing to truly acknowledge Him.

Our oldest daughter graduated from high school with a very high grade point average, which was an advantage while applying for college. We went to visit a few colleges. When we went on these wonderful outings as a family, there was something we were realizing about each one of our children. Some are more stay-at-home bodies while others were ready to take off. Our oldest daughter was a homebody, so she desired to go to a college in the area. It was the same college her grandmother had attended, which was exciting. She also had started working with the Insurance Institute of Highway Safety, which was an excellent job. On her off time, she would sing with the Joyful Sounds a singing group that was started up by some young adults in the church. It was wonderful.

Our second-oldest daughter was preparing herself for graduation and also finding herself with several opportunities that strongly linked into her field of video productions and furthering her education. She developed a Claymation commercial that was aired on PBS. It was called, "Don't let the TV be the babysitter." At the end of the commercial, the television ends up eating the children. Is that not interesting, especially today with over nine hundred channels? Are the media devices swallowing up our children? Just a thought. She also was in show choir and attended the last Macy's Day Parade before 9/11. This was our daughter who, at the age of five, went door to door selling simple rocks, and people were buying them! I can't remember her profit, but it was and still is amazing watching this girl in action.

Our oldest son was struggling somewhat with the transition to public school. I found myself at the school, not in a defensive mode but in a stance of concern. There were no major overall disturbances. It would be concerning his attention in class and things on that level, but I never had to come in for a fight or disrespectful conversations, which would have been grounds for termination in my household.

My husband was working more hours out of the home, and we didn't spend that much time together as a family anymore. I found myself going to church all alone. At one point in time someone asked me if I was a single mother because they had not seen my husband.

When he did find time for the family, it surrounded the children's sports activities. Our oldest was pretty much done in the sports spectrum, but her sister was still going strong in soccer. Our oldest son was in AAU basketball, and he also played soccer. I mention the AAU because of the traveling that was involved.

The little ones had started playing recreational soccer, which took us to another level of busyness, often in separate directions.

We still had our God moments during these times of transition. For instance, there was a day when I was walking with my walking buddy. I saw an eagle and she didn't see it, and I kept trying to convince not only her but my husband and our older children to the point of frustration. I gave up talking about it. One day I felt bold enough to ask the Lord to reveal an eagle not only to me but out in the open so everyone would see it. It was during our prayer time with the family. Well, during a soccer practice, out of nowhere there was a swooshing sound that caught everyone's attention, and I looked and said at the same time, "There goes my eagle! Thanks, God!" My husband looked over at me and just smiled. The kids were pointing and saying, "Mommy, look, it's the eagle." I smiled and retorted with, "Isn't God cool!"

## The Call for Change

During this time, my husband got a call from a prospective business that was out of state. These types of calls were not unusual because my husband would get calls from headhunters at least once every other week with interesting job proposals. The season when the call would come in would determine the attention my husband would give it to the point of even discussing it with me with any seriousness.

At this time in Maryland, I was pretty set in my ways. This was definitely home, and nobody could tell me anything different. Then that one phone call that caused me to recoil into my secret closet. This was the call that came back approximately four months later after reaching out and not really receiving a response from my husband. They offered a better position that would allow him to be home more with not as much travel. With everything that was going on that my husband was missing out on at home, he took this call seriously.

When my husband told me he was going to Virginia for an interview, bells and whistles started to go off in my head. *How dare he!* was all that was running through my mind intensely. Our children were so settled and happy.

One of my biggest concerns was moving Mary away from her pediatricians who had followed her from the university hospital to her pediatrician's office. That was such an awesome moment when we all realized the hand of God with Mary's doctors' transitions and how they ended up in our particular office. One of the doctors actually came to the house and chilled out with us for a while. It was an exciting time as we came together acknowledging the hand of God.

Now our second-oldest daughter had selected a college and had been accepted into their video and communications program at Villa Julie, a private college in northern Baltimore. She had applied as a commuter because we lived about forty-five to fifty minutes away, so it was no biggie. Well, not until the decision of going on the interview came into play. I hope you are feeling me on this one.

He went out on the interview and called me on his way home to say it was interesting and we would see what would come out of this one. Now this was serious. I found myself putting all wheels in a different direction, and it was not appealing to me at all. I found myself truly feeling like Sarah moving away from my homeland, preparing to pick up my tent and move. The scariest part for me was that I really didn't know anyone in this area except one couple we had known for a few years, which made the transition palatable, to say the least.

Through all of these transitions that I found myself sitting in, I knew where to go, and that was my secret closet within me. There are times in my life when I feel as though I will just completely shut down, almost into a catatonic state of mind. What I find to be a peaceful place is my place of focus on the cross and the forgiving love that comes from the one who calls me His beloved. I find myself mentally running to Him for a peace that totally surpasses my understanding. I then find myself getting to walk out my life with confidence in knowing it is for His name's sake that I continue to walk this life out.

The house market was starting to change for the better, and we ended up selling our home within a three-week period of time. This was exciting and stressful at the same time. Having to do the majority of the cleanup and arranging for the selling market and the constant, "Don't sit that there!" became a bit monotonous.

My husband told me originally that this change would not only bring him home but that the gentleman we had known for some time was a Christian. My husband felt as though this was God's way of "iron sharpening iron," as he put it. That was the best thing that I had heard about the move.

**Moving Day!**

The final day of showing our house to the new owner, which we were unaware of at the time, was somewhat of an experience that finalized some issues in my family. The time was intense. We were all under some great pressures, which continued to press us back to a foundation of a belief that kept us together.

It was a normal day of the children returning home from school. I was dealing various details of how things were working out in the arena of closing out certain items and then finding more details that needed to be addressed. Suddenly, the phone rang, and since we were selling the house, we were always on edge when the phone rang. Everyone was in a somewhat of a still position, ready to change direction if necessary. And it was necessary; the real estate agent on the other end of the line apologized for the short notice, but they were around the corner and had just seen the house. They were wondering if they would be able to come in to view it. At this point, in order to stop the madness, any buyer was good. My positive response was a quick one with an imperative of, "Give us about fifteen minutes because the children had just come in from school." Then they were free to come and view the house. It was agreed upon, and then I hung up the phone. This is where the world changed within the walls of my house. My voice went from a soft-spoken individual to a demanding officer, with specific details of direction in play.

My oldest son and second-oldest daughter were in position to take on the orders at hand with the swiftness they had been trained in throughout the previous two weeks. As they scooped up their little brothers and sisters, we proceeded to the car. I then turned the car on with a video playing and the air conditioning running. Then I returned to the house. Now it was my turn to make the home something the perspective buyer would want. I ran from room to room with proficient urgency, flushing all toilets, turning on all lights, and straightening all the linens. It was a flurry of movement with purpose to sell the house.

As I was ending my rounds and coming up from the basement, I heard a loud ruckus coming from a distance close enough to concern me greatly. While I approached the door that was the entryway through the garage, I found a situation that caused me to lose all of my past composure completely. What I saw was my son clutching his sister's blouse, and them both vehemently yelling at each other, while her back was braced up against the wall. I then began to yell at my son and ran toward the altercation. My fists were raised in position to swing on my son without any concern or thought, other than getting him off of my daughter.

At that point my son turned to look at me, not because of the pain from the blows but because of the demeanor that was being exposed out of my anger. Then, knowing that we had to leave before the real estate agent and the prospective buyers showed up to see the house, we stopped. This would not be a very loving impression for anyone to see.

When we found ourselves in the car wiping our faces and straightening out our clothes, the words that followed were the glue that continues to hold our family together. The words were not from textbooks or the inspirational speakers of life. They were and still continue to be the words of love coming out of the word of God. There was a song we would listen to quite often, and the words were scriptural. They went something like this: "No weapon formed against me shall prosper, it won't work. Though the enemy comes in like a flood, the Lord will lift up a standard against it, and it won't work, no, no." The standard of God's Word is what was lifted up in our car on that day, and our house was sold!

Chapter 10

# What Is Temporary?

A s the movers packed up the last items from the house, we knew we were headed toward temporary living for a few months until our house was built. Our second-oldest daughter packed for school and a partial move to Virginia. Our oldest daughter opted to stay in Maryland with a friend temporarily.

While saying all of our good-byes, it was as if we knew these relationships were about to come to an end, especially with my prayer partner. Those were some long good-byes, with great longings for the fellowship to continue. Deep down inside, we felt that it was the end to something to be treasured and remembered as we continued to grow as children of God.

We moved in mid-June of 2001. It was a hot summer down in Virginia. I was just getting over a terrible bout of bronchitis. I later found out that the many daffodils I had planted all around our home in Maryland were the culprit. Little did I know that my new allergy friend from nature was going to be mold and pine trees. You will smell them coming down 95 South; it is very aromatic.

Before we began our search, the Lord had me write out the specifics of what I wanted in our home, and so I did, and that included a basement with a full porch and a first-floor bedroom specifically for our parents when they came to stay. Because of the previous visits, this revision was a no brainer.

Our temporary home was a beautiful little country-style home with a full porch. It was fully decorated with all the needed essentials for a family of eight. It had four bedrooms, two full bathrooms upstairs, and a half bath downstairs. It also had a lot of antiques on display that were pretty to look at, but for the children I had to give them zones.

It had no basement, which I found out was common in the area. There was one issue that was brought to our attention, and that was called the shrink swell soil test. Lots of homes in the area were beginning to have major cracks in the foundations due to the surrounding coal mines that were underground that at times would start to collapse and cause whatever was built on top to start to move and crack. That automatically put us in the new home market when searching for a home. Other than that, we were able to find a wonderful area with a great builder who is still one of our good friends.

As our new home was being built, I found myself over there quite often picking out small details with the finishing touches. It was fun and a little exhausting due to the fact that at the same time I was taking care of school details. Yes, we decided to send all the children to public school. It seemed like the right thing to do with the change of the surroundings. It was a slower pace, and the schools had a different ratio of teacher to child in the classroom. On the average it was one to twenty, which was considerably better than what we had just left, on the average one to twenty-six if things went in your favor.

Mary was the most trying in placing her because she ended up in a different school than her brothers. But all seemed well in Pleasantville as I looked at it from the hustle and bustle of Maryland and DC to the small suburb in Chesterfield, Virginia.

All the people spoke to you with a little bit of a twang in

their voices. I thought it was pretty neat. I believe at times I even slipped into a twang here and there. It was not out of disrespect, but it is something that I tend to do sometimes. The children get after me about it at times, and that is when I bring it into check.

I didn't drive that often because I didn't like getting lost. The most driving I did early on was back and forth to Maryland with the closing of the house and some paperwork details that could only be handled in person because a signature was needed to finalize closure.

I remember one day on September 10 late at night driving down Midlothian Turnpike, which was right around the corner from our house. I passed a car dealership that had a humungous flag flying. It was so awe inspiring to me on that night because, to be very honest, I don't believe I had ever seen such a huge flag flapping in the wind. It seemed like it was going to storm that night, so I was hurrying home from our oldest son's soccer practice. It was a little ominous, to say the least. Little did I know what we were embarking on that next morning.

## What Is Going On?

The next morning, while Morris was preparing to go to work, I said good morning and asked him what time it was. He responded with, "Five thirty-something." I then asked if he had gotten Little Morris up, and he said he was up and getting ready so he could catch the bus. We had some mix ups the first couple of days, so I wanted to make sure we were in right order this morning, and we were. Yeah!

As Morris walked over to the bed, he gave me a peck, and then he would say something like, "Off to make the doughnuts." Before he leaves we make a habit to hold hands and pray, and we did. Then he was off to work, briefcase in hand and cell phone in check, and he went out the door with a final, "Love ya, hon."

That night I did not sleep well because our baby girl, Amaris, was experiencing pain from an ear infection coupled with a slight fever. At this point she was sleeping and her fever was down, which gave me a little boost of energy.

While she was resting, I was able to wake the rest of the crew to prepare them for school. It was a groggy but good morning because on this particular day, it seemed as though we were all moving in the right direction together. The weather was beautiful, a little crisp but clear and just an indescribably beautiful day. Little Morris had made it to the bus stop, and he was off. Mary was next. After checking all three backpacks to make sure all items were in place, I put their lunch bags in with their thermoses. Yes, I was on a roll. All jackets were on the backs of their chairs as they all ate their oatmeal.

Mary's bus came right in front of the house, so I walked her out, said good morning to the bus driver, and then kissed Mary. The bus driver helped her to her seat on the bus. I then waved from the front porch as I proceeded back into the house.

The boys were finishing up with their oatmeal and placing their bowls in the sink. With a little bit of time to hang out before leaving out for the bus, I went upstairs to get their sister, who had awoken and was calling me.

I went in to the room where she was standing up in her crib, reaching out to me with one hand and with the other rubbing her eyes. I changed her diaper and grabbed a blanket to take her with me as we all walked to the bus stop.

We all walked out together. Actually the boys went running, as if they were racing each other, and I had to call out to them to slow down. They slowed down enough for me to pick up with them and then to proceed to the bus stop. At the bus stop there were a few children with their moms since this was only the second week of school.

One mom came out late with her coffee mug in her hand and asked as she approached the corner if anyone had seen the news report on TV about a plane hitting one of the towers in New York. One mom said she had heard something about it, but we all agreed that it was strange. It was handled as if it were something to be cleared up later. Someone even talked of a recent jet that had crashed into a building, and we all remembered that and agreed that it was probably something similar.

At the same time the bus was approaching, so we all said our good-byes and then scampered back to our houses. I remember walking into the house, sitting Amaris in her high chair, and giving her some apple juice to sip on out of her sippy cup. Then I continued in a pattern of cleaning up the bowls and utensils from the morning and fixing Amaris her oatmeal as well. I prepared her amoxicillin for her ear infection and her baby Motrin in measuring spoons for liquid meds to administer them after her oatmeal.

At this point I start to think about what we had been talking about at the bus stop, and I figured I would turn on the news instead of the norm of pushing in a Veggie Tales video.

What I saw on the TV was fear in the eyes of the newscasters. Their conversations were so convoluted that it grabbed my attention. They showed a live video shot of smoke coming out of one of the towers and then all of a sudden something hit the other tower. They were trying to make some sense out of what was unfolding before not only their eyes but mine.

The only three names I recall hearing recanted over and over again were Katie and Tom and Diane, for they were three of the news anchors working on that day.

At this point I had fed Amaris and administered her meds

slowly and methodically while mentally I felt like I was in a cloud of multiple thoughts holding hands with fear.

I grabbed the phone and started dialing. First I tried to get in touch with Chiara, our daughter who was attending college in northern Baltimore, and there was a busy signal. After several times of pressing redial and getting the same thing, I then called Patrice, who was working at a hospital in DC, but it was the same story busy. I then called my husband as I wiped Amaris's face and picked her up. I went to the recliner, which was positioned directly cattycorner to the TV. As I curled up with Amaris and the phone, my husband answered, and I just burst into tears. In a frantic tone with some composure in order not to scare my daughter, I said, "Honey! Have you seen what's been going on!" He said quickly, "Yes, and have you spoken with the girls?" My answer was of course no with an explanation. He explained to me that all the lines were pretty much down, and then he reassured me with a calm, "They should be okay."

Now at the same time all of a sudden the Pentagon was showing signs of some explosion. The news anchors were speculating that this was another plane. At this point I couldn't help it. I screamed out, "Honey, did you just see that? What is going on!" At this point in our conversation my husband told me that he was on his way home. Then he said, "Denise, now is the time to pray, and I will be home soon."

My prayers did begin suddenly with, "Oh, God! Why?" Then my prayers were directed toward my children. I wanted to hold them all at this time, but I couldn't, so I thanked the Lord for doing it for me. I then just sat in that chair almost in a catatonic state. I was holding Amaris, and by this time the Motrin had kicked in and she was sleeping in my arms, which brought on a peace for me at this traumatic time.

As I look back on this time, I know there are many of my faithful readers who are recalling that time on 9/11, which was a time that brought us all together like no other time I could ever remember.

I remember the American flags on the cars. I can recall the conversations with a genuine concern when someone spoke of a lost one or someone who was unable to make it home because all the planes were grounded.

My husband's coworker who was living in the area that was the iron sharpener by faith with my husband ended up stranded in London. My sister-in-law was in Boston. She was at the terminal when the first hijacked plane took off that crashed into the first tower.

We were all affected. I believe like no other time we were experiencing a unity that was surrounded with a grief for an attack on innocent life.

I was reminded of someone else also as those firefighters and police officers went into those burning buildings. They weren't thinking to themselves, *Let's see, I am only here for those who look like me.* Or *I am here for all the Catholics, Muslims, and Christians. Maybe it's the Buddhists. No, it's all the atheists. No, I am here for those who are women. No, it's the men and children. And what about those who are disabled? Well, I think they would just be a burden right now. Let's leave them.*

I don't think they were thinking about medals or recognition. It was all about saving lives without thought of race, religion, age, or abilities. I think they were on a mission for life without taking account for their own lives. They had a tenacity that was felt by us all as we saw those towers crash to the ground. They continued to the end.

After the first tower came down, you would expect for them to come out, but no, they continued for life. May God bless all of those men and women who gave up their lives for ours on that dreadful day that we now have etched in our memories called 9/11.

That someone else I am reminded of is Jesus, as He died on the cross for us all to save all of our lives from death eternal. He did not have to do it, but He did. I call Him Daddy!

I remember a feeling here in America that seemed as though we were all part of one big family. I remember the magnetic flags on the cars and mottos of God bless America or the one I really liked, America bless God.

I felt so blessed to be a part of this people group known as Americans. Whenever I saw firemen or police officers, I was actually talking to them. Before September 11, I would not just start talking with these men and women of service. And any military service people were acknowledged by everyone with gratitude and appreciation that was unreal.

What brought us together was a passion for life and a disdain for the taking of innocent lives. Think about it; that is one thing we all have in common. That is called love.

Chapter 11

# Church (Social to Relational)

I *find myself after the terrorist* attack here in America in search of a people group who truly believe in God. My personal trip into Midlothian, Virginia, was interesting. I had asked both of my pastors from Maryland if they had any recommendations, and neither did, so there I was, a little fish in a fish bowl.

As I was driving to take our son over to his soccer practice one day, I found a church that had a banner outside advertising Awanas classes, and the name of the church was the same as our church in Maryland, so hey, why not? I actually drove over while my son was at practice, and the doors were open, so I went in. There was a worship team inside having a jam session, which was cool. I gave a wave and said, "Hey, we just moved into the area. Your banner actually caught my attention, and I was just wondering, what time is service?" They responded with a time, and I thanked them and went to walk out the door. Then a small box caught my attention. It was a prayer request box, and I thought, *Why not?* My request was concerning my family finding a home church, be it this one or another. I just wanted a home for my family to congregate with other believers.

## Was That You?

After a couple of weeks, we finally went to the church over by our son's soccer practice. It was a contemporary style of service, and they had two services every Sunday, one in English the other in Spanish. We worshiped with them for a few months.

I got the children involved in Awanas, which was something they were familiar with from Maryland, and that was good. They also had a Saturday coffee shop with drama incorporated. I remember one time they asked our oldest son to play in a skit. They wanted him to play the part of Jesus, and our son backed out.

While we were attending that church, there was a time when I ran into one of the members, and of course the thing that stuck out for me about her was that she was homeschooling. In one of our sessions, she was expressing some issues and requesting prayer for them, so we did pray. The next time I saw her was at the YMCA, so as I asked her about her mom. She said she was doing better and thanked me for the prayer. Then somewhere in our conversation, I mentioned something that keyed in to the request that I had placed in the prayer box. She looked at me with astonishment and said, "So, that was you that I have been praying for!" Then it connected; she had picked my prayer request out of the box and had been praying for the no-name person, and here I was telling her the praise report of answer to her prayers for that no-name individual. Praise the Lord!

## Parent Teacher Association

As we were settling into our position in the public school system, I not only signed the sheet during open house night, I actually got involved. I believe it was a little bit of spying on my part, when I could with a baby on my hip. I was able to put papers together for the teacher for handouts and things like that. I was a possible chaperone on field trips and lunch room overseer—little odds and ends jobs like these.

One day while helping with other moms setting up papers for testing, one mom and I started talking, and I was asking her what church she went to. After September 11, you could pretty much talk freely about your faith in Jesus, which she did, so I asked her what church she attended and where it was located. It sounded a lot like my former church in Maryland. She shared positive information with me and encouraged me to come on out because her son and my son were in the same class. I thought that was cool.

By this time, our oldest daughter had decided to move back home and start all over in Virginia, so we went and helped her to move home. We prayed together, and she was willing to trust in the Lord with her life. She found a job and started back to school, which was great! She did go on a little tangent and went and caught a train to Connecticut and then into New York to audition for *American Idol*. She got a chance to sing, but it wasn't her time to shine.

At the same time, Chiara had successfully settled down at school and was striving in her course on campus. On her way to school, she expressed to me some slight anxieties that she could not put her finger on. I said, "Chiara, could it be that it's like, after for so many years of having the principal on the playgrounds and Mom and Dad, from the sandbox to the swings to warn you when you were going too far, and now it is up to you to trust that inner voice and trust Him for yourself without seeing Him?"

She looked at me with a small tear in her eye and said, "Mommy, I am not getting emotional. This is a good move, and I don't want to cry!" This is how we converse in love and understanding beyond words.

Little Morris was playing basketball for the high school, and very often when he came home he did not come by himself. There were the other guys from the basketball team who would gather and play video games and of course eat. They were boys! They all call me Mom, which I think that is cool.

When Little Morris first started school, I wanted him to take his freshmen year over because he was only fourteen years old at the time of admission. They did comply with that, but it put him in a bracket that kept him from playing basketball. I am so proud of our son. He had to basically pass the ninth grade in three months on the Internet and at the same time catch up with his new tenth-grade schedule. And he did it!

Mary was enjoying her new school, and so were the boys. Everyone was doing well, and I was continuing to thank the Lord. We did attend the church that the one mom had invited us to come out and visit. It was just my daughter and me because before everybody else came out to a church, she and I had been church hopping for a couple of months to do a general survey.

## Small Church in the Woods

Patrice and I decided to visit First Baptist Church of Midlothian. Its location was down this back road. Beside a huge tree, there it sat—a little brick church. With its gravel parking lot, we pulled up and proceeded to enter through the front entry doors. As we entered the vestibule, we could hear someone speaking with a few, "Amens."

I felt like I had stepped back in time as the usher guided us into the sanctuary. Long, dark wooden pews in the center flanked on either side, with shorter pews of the same design. What really took me back were the wooden-handled handheld fans, which were very noticeable as they were being used for fanning and with motions of agreements by raising them in the air by several members. Yes, it was a conversing congregation, Amen! It's okay to answer.

We decided to join that church as active members. I started to gain a strong bond with the first lady. She also would have speaking engagements outside of the church, and at times I would go to support her. I examined and especially appreciated her willingness to take on her mom, who was suffering with Alzheimer's at the time.

I joined the choir, and during the summer months I was volunteered by the first lady to conduct a worship class. I agreed to it, but after the meeting I had to ask, "What is a worship class anyway?" This was the start of something in the church that was called the DIG ministry—Dance Inspired by God for the youth of the congregation.

How it all started was during VBS (Vacation Bible School). Actually my two older daughters also participated. Chiara helped me organize a dance for all of the children, and I had the adult class do a dance also. The children did a choreographed dance to the song "It's Rainin'" by Kirk Franklin, and the adults did one to the song "Why We Sing" by the same artist.

At the end of our presentation, I asked to do a personal dance, which incorporated the song that I had listened to as I rode in the back of our van while being held by my mom on that sudden day of Mary's delivery. The title of the song was "Hold Me" by Commission 7, and it had become a personal favorite of mine. What I was displaying before this group was a personal dance that I had only conducted in the presence of my heavenly Father. Immediately after the performance, the whole church stood and applauded. The pastor said to me in the presence of everyone there, "Denise, that was beautiful, and the Lord has placed on my heart that we are to start a dance ministry. It all starts right here." All I could say was, "Thank you, Pastor, and I will do the best I can because this was not something that I took classes for. I will give out what the Father gives to me."

This dance also carried over during a period of time when my parents were going through the seasonal stages of aging, which was causing them to be in a position of needing some assistance. My father ended up in the hospital after a hard fall, which caused a familiar diagnosis to be detected better known as dementia.

After Dad's diagnosis, there were decisions amongst the siblings that we had to make as a family, for our parents living out the rest of their years in as much comfort and stability as possible that we all could agree on. At first I was a little adamant about having my parents to stay with us eight hours away from their home. I had to let go of the rose-colored glasses of being able to take on my parents the way they had taken me on and realized it was best for them to stay in Cleveland under my sister's care. It was the best situation in the end of all our decisions, and I thank God for the growth out of each season of life as we face them with love.

Sitting in the living room of our parents' home on that solemn day, I looked around at my brothers and sisters while coming to a close of decisions with a peace for our mom and dad. I realized that this might be the last time that we would sit together in this living room. I then expressed to everyone that this song that was a favorite of mine called "Hold me", because of the day when Mom held me when we rode in the van to the hospital on the day of Mary's birth. I wanted to share that hug with them in this dance, and they responded positively. I performed the dance, and my dad said, "Girl, where did you learn how to dance like that?" Then he said, "Come here, girl!" He hugged me and said, "I love you, girl." This is a memory held on to ever so tenderly of an end and a beginning.

## Identified by Love not Law

During this season of life, we continued with the dance ministry. That went off well, and the Lord did bless it as the children were coming in ready to seek for the presence of the Lord because it was appealing to them. I love those children. Even today when I see them they still call me Momma T. I continue to remind them of who they are as residents of the kingdom of God and to represent the one who created them and loved them.

One time I ran into one of my adopted children, and he was having a really tough time. I grabbed his hand in order to take something tangible that we could focus on.

I began to talk to him in reference to his individual fingerprint. I asked him, "Is this what they use in courtrooms to identify us in a crime scene?"

He agreed with, "Yes, ma'am," which is commonplace with children down south.

I then responded quickly with, "So your fingerprint is a positive identifier of you, and this is the only one like this one, right?"

He gestured in agreement. I said, "Guess who created you the way you are?"

It was like a light bulb came on in his eyes when he said, "God?"

"Yes! And He did not create your fingerprint for being identified for a crime but because He loves you individually and there is not another one like yours, so continue doing you!"

I told him after that if I ever saw him like that again, I was just going to take his hand and point to his individual fingerprint designed with great purpose as a reminder. I told him I loved him, and he said "Thanks, Momma T." No problem, anytime, and they know that.

**Uncle Tom**

During the spring of 2004, we received a heart-wrenching report of our Uncle Tom's passing. Morris and I were very close to Uncle Tom and Aunt Mable because once a year Morris's family would have a family reunion. It was started by their daughter Edwina, and we tried to make each one. At the family reunions we would find ourselves in conversations with several members of the family, but most often we would find ourselves spending more time with Aunt Mable and Uncle Tom because our conversations would always circle around the glory of the Lord and seeing His hand move in our lives. Their response was always a positive. They encouraged us with the children, and in all honesty, it was not the norm of families to have more than one or two children and to have more than three put you in the, "So do you plan on having your own team!" category of sarcastic remarks.

When we received the news, I immediately said to Morris, "Can we go down, honey?" He responded with, "Sure, we can leave out in the morning and make it down there for the viewing." We also got in touch with Mom and Dad so they knew that we would be coming.

We left early that next morning. While driving down the highway going south, I was in such exuberant praise. My praise was for a brother who was at home, and I felt so strong in this area. My tears were tears of joy for having known Uncle Tom and the time of sharing our lives here on earth in the excitement of assurance we had for each other.

When we reached Camden, South Carolina, we found ourselves on the inner city streets, which led to the funeral home and also their home, which was a few miles away. As we were approaching one of the stop signals, there was a police car with his lights on, and I looked over to see what was happening. I will never forget this moment. What I saw was a man walking down the sidewalk with a huge cross draped over his shoulder.

I said to Morris, "Honey, today is Good Friday, isn't it?"

He said, "I believe so."

I then said, "Honey, I want to walk the cross with that man!"

He knew I was serious, so he immediately put me back into right order as to why we were here and the time that was available for us to share with the family. I was so crushed but at the same time understanding. At that moment I purposed in my mind to make a cross and walk it on Good Friday.

That next year was 2005, and I did make a cross, with my father's work gloves I walked it through my neighborhood with the children. Before I went out, I thanked the Lord for the year before, where there was a great loss in our lives physically but spiritually there was an everlasting awakening. From that year to this date we continue to walk the cross on Good Friday. Our crowd has grown. It now involves my brother's son and his family of six from Pennsylvania. We have such great times greeting everyone we see on that day. It brings on a remembrance of the day that I forgot that it was Good Friday, and it was so refreshing to see that man carrying the cross to remind me as I was focusing on death to remember the everlasting life of love forever!

## There's No Time on Your Sign

We found ourselves leaving our church family at First Baptist of Midlothian in love. There were many changes that were going on, and in order to continue to follow in the way that the Lord was leading us at the time, we finally had to end that blessed chapter of our lives.

I did start to homeschool again, and it was due to the things that were being diagnosed with my boys, like obesity and slow learner labels. I could not stand and agree with them, so we came back home.

It was blessed in so many ways. One way I cannot pass this opportunity to acknowledge was when James and Michael were baptized. Mary was to be baptized also, but she was afraid to go down into the water, so hers was acknowledged in the fact that she had made a decision in her life to acknowledge Jesus as Lord in her life.

Our pastor passed away, and First Lady's mom passed also. These were sad times, but God is already in our tomorrows, so even in those times we continue to trust His Word as author and finisher of our faith.

One Sunday morning, Morris asked me if I wanted to go out for some breakfast, and I accepted his invitation. Can we step to the side here for a minute? When I am not in church on Sunday, I feel out of place, probably from my upbringing, but I just had to be honest with my feelings at this time. We ended up in a diner that was located maybe three miles from our house. Another one of our children's friends worked there, so it was good company.

While sitting by the window, across the street diagonal to the diner was a middle school. Outside of the middle school there was a temporary sign that said, "Open Door Baptist Church, come worship with us!" I mentioned it to Morris, and he said "What time does service start?" I kept looking, and then I said, "Maybe we can read it better outside after breakfast."

We left the diner, and as we surveyed the sign, we both came to the same revelation that there was no time on the sign. At that point, we were discussing the bad advertisement that they had chosen to display for their church. We decided the next Sunday to attend at a time that would be in range of normal church hours around 11:00 a.m. When we came in, there was someone in the hallway who handed us a bulletin, and on the bulletin was the starting time of 10:00. We were going to leave since they were so far into their service. They encouraged us to stay, and we did, for approximately three years.

We did have to tell Pastor that we noticed their sign did not display a time, which was only the start of a great family relationship in Midlothian, Virginia.

While attending Open Door Baptist, the dance ministry continued to flow. I found myself in the choir, which was a blessing also. The congregation was a mix of a conservative relaxed atmosphere with some conversing from pulpit to congregation.

We started going to small groups, which allowed us to congregate in small numbers on a weeknight. It was very similar to the in-home Bible studies my parents would have, which brought back so many good memories. The aroma swirling in the air filled with a rich coffee smell. I remember the sounds of laughter and voices with a standard that we were coming together to spill out and encourage in love. God is so awesome!

During one of our group sessions, we were studying a portion of the Scriptures that has held with me like super glue. It was, "If you abide in Me and My words abide in you ..." (John 15:7). What stuck for me was something our pastor said, who was so cool, by the way, with his guitar in hand as we would go into praise and worship (exciting times!). He elaborated on the word *abide* and asked us to replace it with the word *continue*. Whenever I have a conversation with a believing brother or sister in Christ, we end all of our conversations with "we shall continue," which is a staple in my vocabulary.

There was one session where we got together at another family's home, which we would do every week. This family was a new family, and it was brought to my attention that they were another homeschool family. That's cool and all, but

I tend to feel that at times people feel that all homeschoolers are in the same box. Actually we do have similarities, and we also have some differences because we are all individuals following either the path that has been laid out for us by the Word or the world. I have been on both sides of the track, so I do understand.

This family tickled me because the mom had an inquiry as to the praise and worship involved in the service. As she expressed it, "Does it take all that!" I took this as a little insult, since I was one of the only ones who would participate. It was acknowledged, and some would approach me at times and say it was a good thing. They would express how it made them feel free to raise their hands or even to express an amen every now and then.

This family has become one of our family's closest friends, and it makes my head spin sometimes as to how the Lord takes someone I truly believe I would never have been close to and turns the heart in love. She has been one of my strongest inquisitors, with an understanding as to how and why I continue to stand the way that I do. It has been amazing. Most of her questions in the beginning were in the realm of race out of the world's ways of seeing ourselves. I would and still do challenge her to line it up with the Word. She has also done the same thing with me, and it has been wonderful. She was the one who pointed out a book to me that took me on a journey. It was *One Blood* by Ken Ham. This was a sign of great change in my life going from social to relational with God. It becomes a personal interrogation.

## Growth Spurts

Within this year, our second-oldest daughter, Chiara, got married to Joey in the month of June in her junior year of college. They came to us to discuss what they were planning and said they wanted our blessings. In the beginning, we felt that they should wait out one more year and then get married, but they were pretty adamant, so we gave them our blessings with prayer. Their theme was fishers of men. There were fishing nets hanging from the ceiling in the basement of the church that they were attending. It was really cute. She did graduate, and they are doing well continuing to be a blessing.

At the same time Patrice was involved in a relationship with her future husband and our future son-in-law, Randy. They were going to bless us with our first granddaughter, and now we are the proud grand parents of two beautiful granddaughters (Kayla and London) through their union.

Little Morris was graduating and planning on going to community college and at this time dating his current-day fiancée, Danielle.

The younger four were getting involved in church missionaries. Of course, they were also carrying out the family traditions of the year-round sports. James asked to play football, which I strongly disagreed with, but it all went well. It actually led us into many relationships that enlarged our family in Christ. They also got involved with a Christian sports affiliation called Upwards. Their dad was not too keen on this one because he said it wasn't teaching the children the real sport.

We also got a puppy, my current-day "space invader," Sadie. We got her from the pound, and she is the greatest dog. When we got her, she contracted a puppy disease called parvo. Her whole litter had contracted this disease, and they had to put them all on IVs to cleanse their blood. When we brought Sadie in, they tested her blood for the disease, and she tested positive. About a week later, they called and said, "We don't know what happened, but your dog never showed signs of the disease." They tested her again, and she was clear. They said, "Come and get her out of here!" With excitement, we went to reclaim our miracle dog. The night before we took her back to the pound, we sang praise songs and prayed over her. She was a little freaked out, but hey, whatever works, right!

While integrating ourselves back into the world of homeschool, we found ourselves living in a state that is actually homeschool friendly and the number of families that homeschool is huge. I found this out when I went to the annual HEAV—Home Educators Association of Virginia—convention. It was overwhelming to say the least. Everyone was walking around with these crates on wheels or even suitcases with wheels full of books, tapes, films, games, and flour-making bread machines. There were rows and rows of booths, and everyone had the best creative way for you to teach everything. All kinds of ideas and materials are available right there all packaged up.

We were definitely expanding and growing in all kinds of ways.

## Submission Is the Role

With all these activities, we decided to go on an opposite world vacation to Kiawa Island. We went to take a break from all the changes that were occurring within our family. On the second day, while driving home from the grocery store, ready to stock the kitchen shelves with individual goodies and essentials, we received a sudden phone call.

It was my sister-in-law telling my husband some news that caused us to turn down the music in the car. Morris's skin tone turned a dusty grey. It was like life was being syphoned out of him while receiving the news on the other end of the phone. I immediately felt the need to pray quietly. When he finished the lengthy phone call of questions and answers, he ended the call with a slight pause of silence, which I allowed him to have with no questions. I did ask with a squeeze of the hand in the center of the car, "Is everything going to be okay?" He answered with uncertainty, "I really don't know." After this my husband shared with me that Dad had just experienced a brain aneurism, and they were not sure whether he would live.

My husband was stoic in character. He continued to do things naturally, such as carrying up the groceries with the boys, and then he just slipped back into the master bedroom and started watching TV while sitting on the bed. After putting all the food away, the girls went into their room and started playing with their stuffed animals, and the boys had already grabbed some sort of snacks and were sacked out on the couches in the family room playing video games. I instructed them to keep the noise down, and at the same time I gave them a general idea of what was going on. The boys and I prayed, and then I went and did the same thing with the girls, and all was good.

Whatever food we had gotten, I had put something in the oven for us to eat for dinner. At the same time, I started to pick up around the unit, making loads to wash clothes and linens. In my mind, I was helping in secret, knowing that we were preparing to leave. I had also explained this to the children, so they were prepared also.

When I came into the bedroom and began to shuffle a few things around in order to pack, my husband, with a disturbed look on his face, asked me what I was doing. I told him, and then I even let him know that I had already prepared the children for our early dismissal. What he told me was hard for me to receive, and I will explain why.

What he said was, "Hon, we are not going anywhere. What we are doing is what my father would want us to continue to do. If we leave, it will not change a thing. We are staying here."

That did not make any sense to me, and I just walked away with a voice of irritation, saying, "Fine then!" I proceeded out onto the porch outside the unit, sat down in one of the lounge chairs, and took out my phone to call my prayer partner to tell her about this situation that was totally beyond words for me.

When she answered, I said, "Girl, you would not believe … And with all that I need prayer, and we definitely need to pray for Morris's heart to be changed." She then asked me if I was outside and I said "Yes, why?" Then she asked me if I could see the ocean. Once again, now with a little bit of irritation, I answered yes. She then told me to calm down and to continue looking at the ocean and that we would pray. Well, her prayer and suggestions were not accepted in love. I have to be honest, I was looking for someone to be on my side. I believe I actually hung up on my prayer partner. Sorry, sis.

After my moment of exhaling, the food was ready, so I called the girls to help me set the table so they could eat. I had lost my appetite, and I just could not sit there and eat. I went back to the bedroom after we prayed over the food and grabbed my Bible. I asked the Lord to speak to my heart because this was beyond my understanding. I then started reading 5:22, which not only told me to submit but to adapt to Morris's ways. At this time, I was crushed. The other thing that came across was the selfish way I was thinking about how the family would look at me since we were here on vacation. Well, not really, it was now a sabbatical. It was a time spent out of the natural zone to regroup in right position for the Father to use us not only with the children but with each other. We were edifying the body while building each other up to go in and fight the good fight spiritually.

Naturally and traditionally, getting up and running was the right way. What the Lord showed me was so much greater. It was standing and standing therefore. I did finally submit to looking out at the ocean, not alone but arm in arm with my family in prayer.

Dad just turned ninety years old this year, and he is the perfect picture of health. Instead of trying, let's trust in the Lord and lean not on our own understanding. Acknowledge Him and allow Him to direct your path.

## Believing God

One day in our mailbox I found a piece of solicitation that said, "Come out on a certain day of the week to meet and have a Bible study called, 'I Believe God!'" Oh, yes, God had answered my prayers. I was so excited until I opened the doors of the clubhouse, and there were several women congregated there expressing their excitement with a speaker by the name of Beth Moore. I was so disappointed until I realized that this was where God wanted me to be to set me down personally and give me a talking to.

During this time of Bible study, there was a tragedy in Pennsylvania, and it involved my sister-in-law's nephew. He had a sudden collapse, and it looked very bleak for him to come out of this disease that was moving faster than the diagnosis. My nephew gave me a call, and we began to pray for his healing. He died, and it was as if there was a muzzle put on my nephew and myself.

We just did not want to agree with the final report. At the same time, we came to a realization that our relationship was a little different. We weren't just aunt and nephew. Because of our beliefs in God as our Father and believing His Word so dogmatically, we were more like brother and sister.

Going back to the Bible study group after this, I was a little standoffish. It was hard to just smile and talk about how powerful Beth Moore's message was. It was personal for me, and I could not continue to hold back.

What I wrote in my Bible study book the day after our call are the words the Lord set up for me to hear at such a time as this: "I believe I am who He says I am. Dear, well-beloved children especially dear to God, call on Me and I will answer, and I will show you great and mighty things you know not of. Don't wonder about Me and fix your eyes on Me and hold your respects on the sight of the miracle that took place as My doing." Fix your eyes on your faith and belief to God!

## A Tool in God's Hand

As our homeschool started to take off, I found myself in search of who we were. As I was looking through the mammoth curriculum books, I decided to look in the areas of history, specifically Africa and the Bible. I had a desire to find out the truth from the Word of God. While at the convention, I had picked up the book by Ken Ham that gave clear heritage of all humans and how, from the ark perspective, we were all connected. He even talked about how dinosaurs had to be on the ark, and then he said, "Why would they bring on the ark two old dinos? Wouldn't make more sense to have young dinos?" Wow, that does make sense.

What I also found was a book titled *Return to Glory* that tells about biblical characters, such as the pharaohs and several individuals by name, and even their skin tone is described as shiny. Then there were the individuals who were mentioned on the jacket of this book, like Bill Cosby. It was so exciting to read. I immediately ordered two more books to send to my parents and also to my in-laws. It generated some exciting conversations between us, especially with my dad and my father-in-law. We also shared it with my prayer partner and her husband.

Now I was so consumed with this feeling of coming out of the darkness. I started looking at my children differently.

Really it was more of an appreciation for the gifts truly that had been bestowed upon me for such a time as this. It was ridiculously crazy.

I found a video that went with the book, and the one person interviewed that caught my eye was Dr. Ben Carson. He talked about not looking at ourselves as being the great one but as a tool in God's hand. That now hangs as a banner in our classroom that, when need be, I redirect the children and myself to remember that we are a tool in God's hand.

We were now doing a group class with three other families. We were doing just science in the first year that we joined. Then we expanded it to history and literature. Of course, with this newfound awareness of who we were, I was sharing it with my fellow homeschool friends, who were also taken aback but also encouraged to study as a family of Christ. We have grown closer than you could ever believe. By being a tool in God's hands, it has caused an engrafting of so-called races into real relationships racing together into the loving hands of the one who created us. It is such a blessing that I love sharing.

Morris and I renewed our vows. It was so cool having the children there, and I wore an African garment with a headdress that was my mom's. This was the year of making everything new, even our vows. We were thinking differently about who we were in the eyes of truly believing that He had created us to enjoy this marriage He created.

## Moving into the Original

When we were preparing to move to Virginia, Morris told me to write down what I wanted in a house, which included a basement. When I shared it with the real estate agent, first he said that would be difficult to find because the majority of the homes in the area were built on slabs because of the coal mines and the shrink swell soil. I put my notebook away after he showed us a couple of homes that were basically split-level homes and not really what we were looking for, so we settled for a house that was similar to our home in Maryland without a basement and smaller. I requested for the builder to make an office into a spare bedroom with a closet and turn a half bath into a bathroom with a shower stall. This was in the notebook for our parents.

One day after church, Morris said he wanted to just take a little ride out to take a look at some new home sites out in Powahatan, so I said sure. While we were riding around, we saw some beautiful homes with approximately five acres of land. We decided after coming back home that this was something that we should just pray on before making the decision on looking for the home the Lord placed on my heart to write out with purpose when Morris told me to write it down. We said, "Let's wait on the Lord. When He leads us, we don't feel pressed. We feel a peace of knowing that it is in His hands and not ours."

In the middle of this season, my father became so ill that it seemed like he was going to pass away. I had that urge again of having them come and stay with me, but I did not have a peace with it. I prayed and the answer was in His Word in Mark 10:28–30 where Peter is stating, "We have given up everything," and Jesus replies with, "Truly I tell you, there is no one who has given up and left house or brothers or sisters or mother or father or children or lands for My sake and for the Gospel's. Who will not receive a hundred times as much now in this time houses and brothers and sisters and mothers and children and lands, with persecutions—and in the age to come, eternal life." After taking this in, I felt as though it really did not answer my question. It actually caused me to ask a question, and that was, "Why did You not include fathers?" I received my answer in a way that I will never forget.

While I was sleeping that night, my thoughts were heavy with grief because of my father. As if a bolt of lightning had struck, I was awoken suddenly with an internal beating of a bass drum. This is the only way I can describe this moment of awe. The words I heard were, *"I am"* repeatedly. It was like I was being pinned up against the wall behind our bed. Thoughts that crossed my mind were being answered with, *"I am."* I ended up saying, "Okay! I got it. You are my Father. It does not have to be said; it has to be known. I will trust in You filling in the blanks of my life." At that point I started to sob and say, "I am so sorry, Daddy, for not truly seeing You as my Father forever and ever!"

After this unreal moment in my life, my earthly father and I started to have a different relationship. When he would be talking out of his head, at times my sister would call me and ask me to talk to Dad. I would say, "Dad, what does our Father say?" As I started to quote the Scriptures that would specifically come to mind at that time, it would calm his spirit and he would say, "That's right." Then we would pray.

The original plans of our home were being mapped out, and it was closer to what we wanted than we thought. Then our thoughts were being redirected..

**Kingdom Purpose**

After all of this, the Lord started to redirect me as my thoughts were going through a major overhaul. Our oldest son went through some difficult times because he was getting caught up in some wrong-turn situations. During this time, I talked with my earthly father, and what he said while he was in his right mind was, "Well, some of us get caught." That wasn't what I was looking for, but then it became deeper than that for me when I thought about it.

When I've been caught, I have an understanding of what

is right or wrong. If I don't, things that are wrong can easily become right in my way of thinking.

My mother-in-law and I started to become closer while she was taking care of Dad. Either she would call us or I would call to check on them after Dad's aneurism. Mom and I had some interesting conversations revolving around my dad and continuing to hold on to the faith. My mother-in-law at first disagreed with the homeschooling wholeheartedly, which I understood, especially with her being a retired science teacher. At this time she started to question that, especially since we were dealing with some serious life changes at this time. Mom started to have faith conversations with me because basically that was what had been lived out before her eyes with some of the major decisions in our lives. She was one of the main witnesses. She even said that she thought the way that I was training up the children to truly believe in God and to trust His Word was the best way. My mother-in-law left us in October 2006 after having a fainting spell at her family reunion in Detroit in August. It was drastic and sudden.

Morris went up to Detroit after her fainting spell to help assist with the situation because we thank the Lord that Morris's sister and her husband were there seeing that someone now had to take care of Dad. The family came together when the sudden death happened. Not even two months later, Mom was gone.

My dad was in another hospital in town when Mom passed, and he just started crying. He said that he wished that he could have been there, and he also said they were so good to us. The Thompsons are good people. I just rubbed his back and said, "I know, Dad," as I cried with him.

Eight months later, my father also passed away in May 2007. The last words he spoke to me as he was having a coughing spell. I hated seeing him like that. I grabbed his hand and said, "Dad, are you okay?" He raised his head and said, "I love you," and he then laid back down. Those were the last words heard from that earthly vessel known as Howard Strudwick Beamer.

At his funeral, I announced to everyone that I believe my father's last words were deposited with me so they would not be bottled and capped. Instead they were given to the one who would share them with everyone without being a respecter of persons. From my father to you, I love you.

At this time, I was realizing that I am a representative of heaven. I am a part of a kingdom. Jesus is Lord! I am here to give in a way that is not like the world's ways.

## In the Beginning

In the backdrop of life, we had made a decision in light of all of the changes in the seasons of life with our parents. It was no longer about land but availability to hospitals, and also we must not forget going through the effects of Hurricane Isabelle with all of these life affecting scenarios that were placed before us. We decided to finally move closer in to civilization.

At the time, there was a housing development just around the corner from where we currently lived that was building homes with basements. Since they had now come up with answers to the issues of shrink swell soil, it was safe to build homes with different codes and restrictions on foundations, including plans with basements.

One day Morris and I went into the trailers that were set up for the builders. There were actually two builders within the site that we were considering. I placed before the first builder my plans, and he started showing me his plans. I then responded with, "Thanks but no thanks." The next representative found a plan that they could change to accommodate our plans, so we left and prayed and with a peace, the answer was yes.

These plans were the initial plans that I had written out before we had moved from Maryland that the Lord had placed on my heart. These plans were drawn up with a thought of the life that had been lived and the love that had been extended.

We signed a contract with this company. The property was only three miles away from our other house, which made it very easy to check on progress. From the point of clearing to the building itself was an adventure.

This was all happening when the real estate market was telling us we could afford more, especially at one point in time. Because of issues with the house, we were going to let the contract go and look at some other home sites. We were being persuaded to look at homes that cost almost twice as much as the one we were currently buying. One person said to us that we could actually turn it around and sell it to buy another house of our choice. It was crazy. But the peace was leading us to stay with this house.

One day it became such a pain to stand because of many negatives that were coming out of the buying of this home. We even had to obtain a lawyer to resolve trivial building issues. I went over to the house, and there were roofers putting on the roof shingles. I got out of the car and just knelt down and prayed. When I got up and looked up, the roofers had all stopped working and were looking at me. Some of them raised their hands, and I did the same with a hallelujah. In the front of the house was a lot number with the builder's name, and on the backside I put the words Jesus said while dying on the cross: "Forgive them for they know not what they do." We love you all through our Lord and Savior Jesus Christ! I still have that sign.

To God be the glory! With everything that was going on in our lives, getting the current house on the market was not even on our minds. With everything else going on, we made ourselves available where God wanted us, and it wasn't in putting our current house on the market. It was a thirteen-month process. Houses were popping up all around our house that they continued to stop building, or they would, for example, have the whole house painted yellow with a brick foundation even though we had picked the color gray with stone, all while we were standing there with blueprints in hand.

What God did was when we signed to have the new house built without a contingent sale clause, which put us in the position to buy the house whenever it was finally built. This situation actually kept us from being in a bind to sell our house with any urgency with all the delays that occurred. In turn when we did finally put our house on the market, it sold within a week. God knew it all from the beginning.

## Shalom

As we were going through transitions with Mom's situation, I had been reading a book on kingdom principles that I had bought because of the writer, Dr. Myles Munroe. What he was saying about who we are in the kingdom and kingdom principles was falling in line with where I was spiritually, and I was ready to receive. While our son was going through his turmoil's, Dr. Myles had come into town. At the time we had out of town guests and I was in a, "I don't care" mood. I told my guests, "Whether you want to go or not, this is where I am going with my children, especially our oldest son." They agreed to come, stating that this guy sounded interesting. After attending this church where he spoke, there was such an anointing in their praise and worship. It was refreshing to have a place where I could go and not offend anyone.

While we were being engulfed with such intensity, I needed to find a place where I could go and praise the Lord without feeling as though I had to cut it short in order to not offend anyone. Pastor even came to the house, and we talked about it when he actually came over because of what was going on with Morris's mom. Pastor wanted to pray with Morris and to let him know that he was in his corner. It was a sad occasion, but he let us know that at any time we could still come back home to worship with the family.

At this time, we began to worship at Faith Landmark, which was a huge church with a large congregation that was high in praise and worship. It was very similar to my original home church in Maryland. If you didn't converse in this congregation, it was not the norm. It was good to have a place to praise the Lord through the storms.

Finally, my mom did come to stay with us, and it was a wonderful time of regenerating a relationship with my mom and my sister, which was so peaceful.

I thought it was so interesting while my mom was there. We got to sit together quite a bit and talk and laugh and even cry.

We had a mini reunion with my brothers and their wives. Some of her grandchildren came with their children. My cousin came with her husband. It was a time to reflect and to be strengthened. My sister had gone out on foot and obtained pictures of headstones of our father's father and his brother. I displayed a copy of a letter that my father wrote to his brother while in the South Pacific during WWII. There was also a picture of my mother's mother's headstone.

While Mom was with us, I thought it was so interesting when I asked her, "Mom, was there really a worldwide flood?" She looked at me with a questionable look and said, "I don't know, was there?" I smiled and said "Yes, Mommy, you don't have to question God's Word. It is the truth." She giggled a little and said with confidence, "You're right, girl!"

At the same time in small increments I was looking over curriculum for school for the following year. I came across a video that was called *The Real Uncle Tom*. This really piqued my interest. I ordered it, and it came while my mom was still staying with us, so I figured it was for the viewing later, when mom went back home. Within a day or two of me receiving the video, one of the homeschool moms called me. I had to remind her that I was spending time with my mom and I would be able to regroup in a couple of weeks, so we scheduled a time to meet.

Before Mom had left, my prayer partner came down with her mom. Her mom has been living with them now for over fifteen years, and she is in her nineties. My son said the other day the one thing Mom Carole told him that he will never forget was to keep moving your legs. We played cards, and it was hilarious. Mom Carole would just laugh, and Mommy would start to get upset. They were a hoot together.

After Mom went home, there was an emptiness in the house. Our dog Sadie took it the hardest. She would sit in places where mom would sit.

I did finally get a chance to view the video, and it was very enlightening. It was about a man named Josiah Henson who was the original Uncle Tom. He did not die, though. He ended up in Canada, and he lived a pretty decent life.

When I finally met with my homeschool buddy, she and I together witnessed the hand of God. Here is what happened. She is the organizer of the group, so in her partitioning out of detailed jobs, she asked me with some hesitancy if I would be willing to teach from the literature piece *Uncle Tom Cabin*. At that moment I said, "Stop it, Ginger, you did not just ask me if I would like to teach *Uncle Tom's Cabin*." At this point she was feeling more confident with her request, and that is when I told her about the timing of everything, from the buying of the video and watching it, which prepared me to overwhelmingly say yes. Right then there was not another book I wanted to read more than *Uncle Tom's Cabin* because I had a different understanding of the book than before the video.

*Uncle Tom's Cabin* was a banned book in my house when I was a little girl, so I had a fear of reading it, and if I did read it, I already had preconceived notions about it that would taint my mind. This was a book that was written to expose the evils of slavery to the world, which it did. Not only did it do that, but it also exhibited a people group who were accepting their positions in the kingdom here on earth. A people group was being chained and whipped and still standing in love and praying for their brother to come home and to come out of that dungeon of hate.

This was a shalom period of time as we came together as one with this book called *Uncle Tom's Cabin*. It was like a new awakening.

## I Am Clapping for the Hand of God

It was now the year 2008, and we are thanking the Lord for this time that drove home thoughts.

Early on in February, we went to a convention that Ken Ham was speaking to homeschoolers at a church by the name of Grove Avenue Baptist Church. This was the guy who wrote the book *One Blood*, which gave me clear understanding of who we were from the Bible. After he had finished speaking, he hung around for questions and pictures, and when it was my turn I told him, "I thank God for your dad." He basically turned on his heel and said with a surprised look, "You read my book." I said, "Yes I did." I told him about how his dad made me think about my dad, who stood on the word no matter what. He then looked at my daughter and said, "Is this your mother?" with his Australian accent. She said yes. He then said, "Young lady, you are blessed to be raised on the Word of God."

By the way, Ken this one's for you in agreement and to

all my readers of course, the cover of my book is my father's Bible.

Something grabbed my heart during our election season when I saw one of my pastors from Maryland walk across the pulpit and announce that this was the first time in history that he would have the opportunity to vote for an African American president. At the same time, it was as if I could see Jesus walking with his hands held out, saying, "And what have I done to free you?"

After having Mary at twenty-three weeks and seeing a life redeemed (my own)and then coming out with a knowing of I am loved, I will continue to stand and applaud the hand of God who turns the hearts of men while I stand in defense for life, especially for the weakest of these, the unborn. The most dangerous place to live in the world today is within the womb.

I continuously thank God for His hand that created me. I believe His Word from the beginning coming to an understanding with a peace, wholeness, and knowing who I am in Christ Jesus sitting at the right hand of the Father. I am blessed in the city, blessed in the field, and blessed when I come and when I go. I applaud the hand of God, for He has done great things. My race has already been won. All I have to do is stand. "We shall continue being a tool in the hand of God."

Chapter 12

# *What Is Truth?*

*The morning after the Trevon* Martin shooting was at a high point of media acknowledgment, I found myself filled with emotions and thoughts. My thoughts were screaming at me with such intense volume that I had to write them out immediately. These words I truly see as inspired by God from my life and the studies with questions that were answered through the Word of God.

Good morning. My thoughts won't let me rest, so I just had to sit down and write them out. My thoughts were geared toward us as a people group and our perspectives of ourselves. Let's look at it this way: thoughts become words, words become action, and actions become character. Our thoughts here in America change as we continue to write our own Bibles, meaning books that we consider to really hold the truths we believe as a standard of a right or wrong depending on what stage of life we appear on today. (New script, new character.)

There is a scale of rule called the rubber band standard. This particular rule can be adjusted depending on the degree of what is considered to be a truth at a given point in time. For example, my base of truth says up is down or hot is actually cold. When a standard of truth is taken and adjusted due to the circumstances to fit the thought perspectives of the people group's general worldview at the time, the standard of truth can then be twisted to fit the times.

I see it this way: Say my house is built on a standard of rule that fluctuates depending on who is carrying out the plans today on their terms of a true standard of rule for the day (i.e., twelve inches today becomes eighteen inches tomorrow). Don't be surprised when the winds come in and a little turbulence shakes the foundations of this house. It just might find its way to the ground. I would like my house to be built on a standard rule that does not change so I can stand on a solid foundation regardless of the surrounding forecasts of the weather of the day.

I have found truths in a Creator of words and all human beings, who have the ability to respond to the words, with a freedom of choice being acknowledged. Carpe diem, seize the day, for there are only two things that are not chosen, and they are life and death.

When Jesus stood before Pilate before His flogging and crucifixion, He was asked in John 18:28–40. After Jesus' witness to Pilate of His kingdom and to the question of, "What is truth?" and it has been answered to those who recognize His voice. The best reenactment of these specific words from Scripture is found in the movie *The Passion*. If you have it, I suggest that you watch this one specific scene and let the Lord who loves you speak to your heart as He has to mine.

Where did words originate? I believe that in the beginning was the Word and the Word was with God and the Word was God. With all that being said, there is one word that fascinates me: *heart*. Have you ever looked at it with the thought of words coming from God?

Let's dissect the word for a minute. In the middle of the word there is an ear to hear. Even if you cannot hear, there is an inner ear of knowing. At the end of the word, there are three letters that spell out the word art. Take a look around you and see what you can see. Observe, which is the term used for what we call the study of science. You will see the works of God all around you.

So now we have an ear in the middle to hear and art at the end to be envisioned with the naked eye or with some assistance up close or far away. Who is in the beginning? If we choose to acknowledge Him, it is God. He stands at the beginning, waiting to be acknowledged and heard and seen with all the displays He has created. But wait, if we don't believe that He is in the beginning, then how can we believe that He sent His only begotten Son to finish the whole heart of the matter (H-E-A-R-T)? Jesus did say, "I came to give you life and life more abundantly." Life starts at the beat of the heart, but the mind is the first organ to develop. And that is truth. Think about it.

## What Is the Brain?

Speaking of the mind, a very well-known brain surgeon by the name of Dr. Ben Carson has a belief system that we were all created by God and did not evolve. I thought to myself, *If one of the top brain surgeons in the world seriously believes human beings were created and did not evolve, I have to investigate what causes him to take on this belief system so strongly.* What it boiled down to was that his belief system came out of the same words as my belief system and that was in the beginning was the Word and the Word was with God and the Word was God. I have since read basically all of his books, and his views continue strong, following a belief system of being created by the hands of God and acknowledging Him as his Father. Awesome!

I listened to a speaker one day by the name of Dr. Caroline Leaf. She wrote a book on the positive and negative firings of the brain and how the brain fires upon receiving different impulses and how the brain responds. I thought the intricate details of the brain and the similarities to trees with branches in our brains were quite interesting. The negative tree is the one that is toxic. When you examine it, you find there are actual thorns on the branches. With every thought that is allowed to encamp in the brain that causes negative firing, the tree will continue to grow. Stress is a chemical created by negative thought, such as worry. The amazing thing to think about is the fact that we can think about what we think about. Within the brain, God has created us with a amygdala, which is like a library room for us to pick and choose whether we are going to check this thought out for viewing and contemplating or to put it back or completely let it go.

## How Did We Live so Long?

Surprisingly, speaking of stress and worry, scientists have found that our DNA cord has an end tip like a shoe string tip. Worry and stress cause the tip to erode and unravel, allowing aging and sickness to occur more rapidly. No wonder Melchizidak walked on the earth for such a long time. He had a peace in knowing that the God who kept him on the ark was the same God who was keeping Abraham.

I know you are probably saying, "Wait a minute, there was no one on the ark by the name of Melchizidak," and you are right! However, I found some things out while studying. Let's see if you come to a different conclusion. There was a man after Noah in the Bible who was the oldest person living on the earth. He was six hundred–plus years old. No one at Abraham's time knew of his lineage so far as a mother or a father. He was respected as the high priest of the Most High God. On a timeline of chronology from Adam, I found that Shem was still living in the days of Abraham. There is documentation through the Hebrew ancient writings that also name Shem as Melchizidak. This is just an observation I lay out for you to think about and study. Shem, in his six hundredth year of life, knew the God who kept him saved him and delivered him as they obeyed His Word. There was a life at the end of that rainbow, and he was living it. His DNA strand was not unraveling. It was pretty tight. So was his great-grandfather's, Methuselah. Makes you think just a little.

As for me, this last statement on Methuselah made me think, which causes me to go on a tailspin of research to see what happened to that people group and their fossils. My foundations do start with questions coming out of a foundation of truths from the Word of God. First the people groups who lived during the post-flood era lived much longer than we do (e.g., Methuselah living some nine hundred–plus years). I believe they lived a little bit longer than we do today.

There was a book written by an author by the name of Jack Cuozzo who went from an orthodontist to an ancient curator. His book is titled *Buried Alive*. His studies started with his curiosity coming from the truth. He had an understanding of the dental perspective of aging in man and the changes in today's way of studying our makeup orally. His path crossed with a study that was done at Case Western Reserve in Cleveland, Ohio, in 1928 concerning aging and the effects on the skull called the Broadbent-Bolton Study. It basically lines up with Jack's studies of the pre-flood Neanderthal. I thought this was interesting, and it actually lines up with the truth.

## A Butterfly? Why Not I?

Speaking of Methuselah, there is a generation of butterflies that live for nine months and migrate from the areas around the north in Canada and the northern hemisphere of the United States. They travel down to Mexico, and they all congregate in the same area. None of these butterflies were given a tour guide on their travels from previous butterflies. They just innately know how to get there from their inner makeup, which came from the original Creator. He shows them where they are to go and live in a process of life. There was no school for the butterflies to be trained. The three generations that follow this generation will only live for at the most four weeks.

As I think about this specific insect having an individual code and markings, I think about myself as an individual. I was created with a purpose out of what I cannot see. I became an individual with a brain to think and figure things out, a singular fingerprint with a specific DNA order for a specific time with a definite purpose. So were we all, and I think that is beautiful.

During what we call a dark period of our history in America, better known as slavery, words were put into action. In the mid-1800s, slavery was becoming a catalyst for destructive behavior. There was a Bible to be recognized as the book of truths. It was implemented in the schools to train the children up in that generation of a right or a wrong standard. Where sin abounds (i.e., slavery) Grace abounds more in the Word of God. Grace is the divine influence upon the heart, and its reflection on life is observed in this natural world. Think about it.

Two of the favored books of education used in this time period were the blue back speller and the New England Primer, which both contained references to the Bible as bases of truth. I currently own these books, and it is amazing to me how much the Word of God was implemented within the pages of these books for the children.

## The Word Printed for Common People

Before Europeans arrived to the Americas, there was a great movement for the writings of the Bible to be translated so it could be read by all English-speaking people groups coming out of Europe. It started with a man by the name of John

Wycliffe who was a well-learned man out of Oxford University. He is also well known as the morning star.

Coming out of the Renaissance period was Desiderius Erasmus, who had an impact on Wycliffe through his education through Oxford University. He was immersed in the writings of the New Testament in the Greek text, which also led to the printings of the 1611 King James Version. Wycliffe was born in the year 1330 in Yorkshire. In his lifetime, there were several upheavals in the people groups of Europe. Most of the schisms were drawn from the fallout of many disastrous episodes, such as the Black Plague and the Great Fire that destroyed most of London. There was the One Hundred Years' War and the Peasants' Revolt. The people groups were growing quite weary, and they were looking for solutions, from fruitless traditions and from pure physical hunger for a life outside of what they were experiencing at this point in time.

John Wycliffe became a tool in God's hand as he was led by his passionate desires to see all men draw nigh to the one solution that was known to him as the absolute truth of all queries. The only way to obtain this was through the Word of God. This time period was called the Reformation Period because minds were being reformed. Where the mind goes, the man shall follow.

During this period of time, there were many transitions. There was Martin Luther (1483–1546), who was moved in an uncommon way to achieve this pursuit to allow the more common of people in Germany to read the Word of God for themselves.

The Guttenberg Press (1440) took the handwritten Bible into a whole different realm. The Guttenberg Bible became the first book printed in the world. Prior to the use of the press, it took at least one year to complete one book by hand. As a result of the ability to produce Bibles in mass, there was the potential to put the Word into the hands of the plowman nearly 150 years after the death of Wycliffe. This was the strong desire of a young man by the name of William Tyndale (1494–1536). While all of this was occurring, there was a movement of people groups who were being encouraged through a sense of understanding who they were according to the Word of God instead of the culture that surrounded them. There was a fever in the land that was spreading.

## Now We Can Relate

In 1677 there was a book written out of a relational way of reading the Word of God in a common man's way of understanding: *The Pilgrim's Progress* by John Bunyan. It was written out of his jail cell as a story to be shared initially with his daughter, who was blind. She would visit him almost daily, and he prepared this work for her pleasure out of the simple heart of an understanding of the salvation to be obtained through the travels of Christian, the main character. This book continues to be a top seller today. Within the pages of this book, it states that Christian is carrying a great burden, which is the knowledge of his sin.

As George Washington Carver once said, "When you can do the common things of life in an uncommon way, you will command the attention of the world." John Bunyan was a common man preparing a story for his daughter to give her a hope. Out of his common actions of passion for his child came forth *The Pilgrim's Progress,* which gained the attention of the world.

People groups earlier in this period sought a place to pilgrimage physically. In a way it parallels John Bunyan's relationship with his blind daughter, going to a place and sharing this way of standards that were being sought after as an absolute standard for true life. They were blinded with desolation coming out of wars, plagues, and fires and were on a pursuit to save their lives and live according to a truth, which they now could read for themselves. These were the Pilgrims who landed in America in 1620 with the Geneva Bible in hand with a pursuit for life in the Word.

The Pilgrims had a strong inward desire to share the gospel with a people group they had only heard about but never knew. They started out as Puritans which was an insulting term and they became Separatists because they separated from the Church of England. From 1588 up to the time of their pilgrimage to the unknown world, they found themselves in Leiden for twelve years under the leadership of John Robinson, who loved them and taught them through the Geneva Bible.

The Native Americans, who were known as Indians, were the indigenous people group of the land to which the Pilgrims were bound. The term *Indians* came out of Columbus's explorations in 1492 of seeking out the New World. He thought he had landed on the other side of the world in India (i.e., Indians).

Out of this movement came a writing of another book written by John Elliot, assisted by John Sassamon, a member of the local tribe. He was an elite individual in both societies in Massachusetts. It was actually the first book written in America. It was the Algonquin Bible in 1661. It was written for the people group in their own language, with their culture and understandings being acknowledged. There were fifteen hundred copies made with a printing press that was brought over to assist in the distribution.

The Algonquin tribe was the same tribe that Mattoaca, or should I say Pocahontas, who was known in the tribe as the one who came to know a Creator through her understandings as she was introduced to the Word of God. This led to a symbiotic relationship, enabling the Jamestown explorers to become the first successful settlement here in America.

Something to think about is what caused these people groups to come together and find themselves vulnerable one to another without some sort of faith on a controlling basis?

## What Method Do You Use?

A movement of people called the Methodists began, and they were called this because of their unorthodox method of preaching outside the church walls. Ordinary men would stand up and speak from their hearts about how the Word of God had transformed their lives. They were willing to risk their lives to spread it among the common people groups who surrounded them. At this time of awakening (1703–1791), a man by the name of John Wesley and his brother Charles were immensely involved.

## African Slaves Are People

At the same time, a man by the name of William Wilberforce (1759–1833) in England was being driven through the political realm to see the injustices that were happening to created individuals (i.e., African slaves). They were being treated inhumanly and not acknowledged as human beings.

There was an individual in the camp of Wilberforce's by the name of Olaudah Equiano who wrote his autobiography, which became a big seller. It illuminated a human experience, which was a place that was not being felt from the perspective of the African slave until it was acknowledged through his eyes as an actual victim of the Atlantic slave trade.

Olaudah shared his story from his separation from his princely status in his homeland and his separation from his sister, which was heart-rending. He magnified his relationship with one of the master's sons, which began his understandings of this culture of the unknown. He found himself teetering between two belief systems, Islam and Christianity. After studying for himself, he found what he was looking for in the one who created him with a purpose and a relationship, which he also shared in his autobiography.

In England during this period of time, William Wilberforce

was continually going before the House of Commons with the goal of abolishing the slave trade. Through his counsel with John Newton concerning a choice of whether to stick it out or turn to the church with his passions, he was directed to stand in his beliefs while in politics, so he did.

**Truly Amazing!**

An interesting thing I found out about John Newton was that first he was a slave ship captain who discharged himself from his duties. He became somewhat out of sorts because of a haunting of the no-name slaves that he could not get out of his head until he had an account written up after he became blind. He handed this account over to William Wilberforce. He also wrote a well-known song called "Amazing Grace," which in the Library of Congress. The music has an author John Newton, but it is unknown who wrote the melody. It is a known fact that the slaves came over with a melodic scale called the Pentateuch, and the melody of "Amazing Grace" was written with this scale. This is truly a song that I think about with a feel of the "Amazing Grace" that made it what we now sing today, at times with great emotion.

I actually have one of the oldest instruments from the Ghanaian tribe and it is amazing all these notes produce the melody of Amazing Grace, it's just awesome thank you Dad for all mysteries being uncovered.

**Being a Number without a Name**

The Atlantic slave trade did not begin in 1619 in America, which was the way I used to think until I studied this period of time for myself. Actually it began in South America in 1575, where slave ships were shuttled directly between Angola and Brazil as a part of the sugar cane economy. Out of 10 million Africans taken from their homeland, 9,500,000 were transported to South America and 500,000 transported to America. South American slaves were treated harshly, and a large percentage of them died under extremely brutal conditions. They were viewed as expendable.

While examining slavery here in America, I discovered it did not begin with John Rolf and Pocahontas in 1619. The Native Africans were bought to serve here in America. There was a question about the sale because this people group's entry had not occurred here in America. At this time in America, there was a system of indentured servitude that involved a seven-year service for passage to the New World, and then you were free. In 1640, there was a failed attempt of escape by a man by the name of John Punch who was a black indentured servant. He ran away with two other indentured servants who were of the lighter pigmented people group by the names of James Gregory and Victor. After being captured, James and Victor were given four more years of servitude, while John was given a lifetime sentence to servitude, which is the first actual documentation of lifetime servitude due to a darker pigmentation here in America.

## What Race Are We Running?

Slavery on any given Sunday morning was determined to be right or wrong depending on the orators' passion on that particular morning. It was considered in the Northern States to be wrong. Starting in 1774, in Rhode Island slavery was constitutionally abolished by the state. In a large majority of the Southern churches, the Bible was used as a justification of continuing a way of master over slave mentality.

The main people groups of Americans in the mid-1800s who were given the freedom to read were the majority (European people group). I have to stop here and explain something. When I say people group, I personally am destroying a way of thinking and training myself to think differently. There are different cultural backgrounds that cause us to culturally see and respect things from a different perspective. (In two races, one is running away from the truth and the other is running toward the truth.)

There is still a plantation in the mind breeding an enslavement of untruths, which in turn keeps us bound to a pattern of living by works. It is a constant battle. I as an abolitionist of the mind walk in saying, "Step out and believe the Word of God." If you do, I can guarantee a life that will be beyond what you ever dreamed, even in the difficult times. Do the uncommon and walk away from the world's ways mentally and relax, relate, and release, for you now have a new master who says, "Live your life abundantly!" Ready, set, go!

**Trusting His Voice**

What I have come to understand in my short lifespan is that we must continue to do common things in ways that stand out. One example of this is a scenario in the Bible when Peter and the disciples are in a storm on a boat. They look out and see a figure out on the water, and they believe it to be a ghost. Their initial reaction is fear, but then they realize it is Jesus. Peter looks out and in a very uncommon way, just steps out on the waters. He is willing to no longer rely on who he is and acknowledges and trusts His voice. Understanding Jesus' words, Peter starts walking on the waters—not just any water but turbulent water. Once he takes his eyes off of Jesus, no longer trusting those words but acknowledging his own abilities, he looks at the troubled waters he begins to drown.

I believe that as we are drawn by the words of love that have been saved up for us today to recognize or reject to have a relationship with the one who created us with purpose, we too will stand out and become the uncommon in the common world. We will be able to do the common act of being able to walk on the water and look straight ahead. We can do it in a way of looking to the one who created us and believe His Word, not our abilities out of the uncommon way. That will command the attention of the world.

Chapter 13

# One Little Lost Princess

While *watching the movie The Little Princess*, with Shirley Temple as the child star, an awakening occurred for me. I was watching a little girl whose father in the beginning of the story is being recognized as a highly influential individual. He had a lot of money. At the climax of the story, Sarah, the little princess, finds out that her father has supposedly been killed while at war. She denies this as a truth even though all of her belongings are striped from her. She no longer has a place at the table. Her role has changed dramatically. She now carries out the image of a slave girl physically, but mentally she holds on to a truth that her father is not dead and that she still is the princess. In the end, her father is alive, and all is retrieved.

The awakening came out of a life of a child by the name of Sarah Forbes Bonita. She was discovered by a Captain Forbes of the British ship called the *Bonita* in the 1850s.

At the age of eight years old, Sarah, as she was named by Forbes, original name unknown, had been captured by an African tribe in Nigeria that was still participating in the slave trade. However, at this time England had abolished slavery and was trying to enforce these new terms at other seaports. The king of the tribe refused and offered Sarah as a gift to Queen Victoria. Sarah had been stripped from her tribe. Her parents were killed, her title as a princess was stripped from her, and then she became a no-name individual. Sarah was received into the palace by the queen and raised as a part of the family. The queen sent her to Sierra Leone for some missionary schooling and to keep her from becoming ill. Sarah came back with an awareness of who she was, and it was seen in the way she continued to carry out her life, not as an outsider but with confident affiliation to the queen.

In representation of the kingdom, after the birth of her daughter, she asked the queen if her daughter could be named after her and if the queen would become her child's godmother, which the queen accepted.

Coming back to the movie, there is a scene of Sarah running toward the hospital that has been blocked off, and no visitors are able to enter. She found her way into the hospital, and after continual encounters with authorities, she found herself in a room with Queen Victoria.

The queen questioned her behavior, and Sarah told her that she was looking for her father. The queen then gestured to one of her guardsmen to take her to find her father. Sarah found her father, and he was delirious. The only thing that he said continuously was her name, Sarah. He did not recognize at first who she was, but as the scene continued, after her outburst of tears and frantically stating, "Father, you do remember me," he came to an awareness of who she was.

The awakening was of two individuals named Sarah, one fictitious and the other very real, and Uncle Tom, who was also real. They all had their identity stripped from them by the worlds ways, but they continued to live out who they believed themselves to be with a father who they find out loves them and they retain their crowns.

We all must look at ourselves as being created by God. The fact is that in His Word is stated that before I was in my mother's womb, I was in the hands of God. We are all fashioned from the hand of God with a great plan. Let's not allow the dictates of this world to continue to define us. Let us define ourselves as the children of God and claim our position through the redeeming blood of the last Adam (Jesus Christ) to put us in right relation with a right mind as His princes and princesses, representing His kingdom.

Chapter 14

# Scales Taken Away

During the mid-1800s a book was written, and it got a lot of attention not just here in America but all over the world. It was *Uncle Tom's Cabin,* a book largely misunderstood in America, written by Harriet Beecher Stowe. Harriet, the daughter of an abolitionist preacher, often traveled with an older male relative who had some acquaintances down South, across the border. She observed numerous lifestyles. While perched on porches of numerous plantations, she recognized a pattern of life.

As life continued, she observed life as it was being lived out surrounding her. At a point in her life after she got married, she lost a son shortly after birth. The relationship of life emotionally gave her a thought of passion that caused her to write with a fiery pen. She discovered for herself that God created us all, whether we recognize it or not, and there is a purpose for every life to be respected as a life, including her son's, which can be recognized today as insignificant and short lived.

Life respected, life changing, life leading. This became her driven passion. Her thoughts, her words, her actions, and her character were revived. Harriet Beecher Stowe stated that it was God who wrote the book, which I personally have to agree with as I continue to write knowing that this also is a book that was finished from the beginning by my Father.

As she sojourned, she came across some writings that matched up with the pattern she had witnessed while perched on many plantation porches, and she was continuing to investigate. It was these articles that were written by a man by the name of Josiah Henson. She took his writings, which depicted that he was forced to live within the system of slavery and how it affected him. In her book, she takes some of his accounts and meshes them with many others that were quite similar.

Back then there was an African people group who believed what they were hearing, which was the Bible. A large number of this people group could not read, but they could hear. It was the Word of God that was being read, especially by the children. They believed their names were written in God's book and would not be erased. The main beating scene in *Uncle Tom's Cabin* where the master Legree is beating Tom literally to death, what we see expressed with a continual stance is a belief that many times caused slaves' masters to become even more enraged. That caused them to lose all control as they were beating these individuals because they would not bow down. In their character, they held on to a truth until death.

They believed who they were in the eyes of their Creator enough that they would stand after their beatings and state, "Aren't I your brother and sister in God's eyes?" They continued to pray heartfelt prayers of forgiveness and for a turning of the hearts by the hand of God. They were not only thinking of themselves but of the generations to come as they continued. And the truth will make you free.

Chapter 15

# Character of Tom

I *traveled to Boston recently, and* as I stood there in Faneuil Hall, it was as if I could just step back in time to when that hall was jam packed with many Abolitionists listening to a speaker who was once a slave himself. His name was Frederick Douglas. While speaking at one of his speaking engagements, he singled out a book that he had currently read and said it was a well-written depiction of the conditions the slaves were currently living in. He gave the book high praise. He found himself in the double standard because Uncle Tom laid down of the garments and did not fight. He talked about that in a speech he gave to the Black Regiment during the Civil War. He paralleled the two while encouraging the troops to go out and fight. He then found himself standing so ardently with the book that he was willing to stand in as the figure of Uncle Tom for an event. After these speeches, his words were taken by the *Liberator* and twisted to seem as if he spoke of the character Tom with a double standard, which was untrue. From there it went out as a way of disrespect to be used as a laughing matter of cowering, and that was so far from the truth. He also wrote a personal letter to Harriet, and he ended it with, "I am most truly your great friend." I hope that going back to the origin of a thing helps to clear up some misunderstandings so we can actually take in some of the truths and the way they were being lived out with boldness.

As an individual character, Uncle Tom in the book was heavily mocked in this setting of the master-slave mentality, right down to the beating scene. This character was displayed in theatres in the early 1900s as an individual to be ridiculed for backing down and not standing up. Specifically, in the book at the time of the beating scene with Tom, he spoke words of blessing, which some took to the theatre and expounded on as a springboard of cynicism toward this individual's character.

Out of this scene and others there was a thought that was twisted, especially in the African American people group. The thought that was birthed was, "I am nobody's Uncle Tom." The perspective was twisted, and so were the people groups because as the man thinketh, so is he. The African American group started now running toward a new promised land, which was actually leading us to bondage in the mind away from the thoughts of who we were in Christ, according to the Word of God. Uncle Tom spoke words of blessing, which some took to the theatre and expounded on as a punkish way of responding, not standing up for what is wrong.

It brings to mind for me a time when I chose words of love instead of hate, even though it seemed justifiable. It was a situation where my neighbor (of a lighter-pigmented people group) would release her dog off its leash and allow it to use my yard as his bathroom.

I called out several times from the back deck, and at this point she or her husband would respond by calling their dog, putting his leash back on, and continuing their walk. On one of these memorable days, never to be forgotten, the children and I were about to go to the library, and lo and behold, who's out back! I proceeded to the car with the children, drove around the corner, and stopped the car. I finally found myself face to face with my neighbor. I confronted her about our little situation, and she looked at me like I was crazy and said, "I don't know what you're talking about. That never happened." Out of anger, I wanted to verbally or physically respond in a way that would have been totally negative. From within me came the words, "God bless you," and I had to choose to say these words.

Later that day, there was a knock at my front door. It was my neighbor's husband dressed in his work attire with gun on his hip to tell me that he wanted me to know that the words I chose to say to his wife—"God bless you"—were like curse words to her. He then explained to me about how they had lost a child. He said, "That is not a blessing, so please don't say those words to my wife ever again."

Yes, I was in shock, but about one year later as I was walking our new puppy in the neighborhood, who did I see but my neighbor and his dog. Of course I immediately started to position myself on the other side of the street when he called out to me in gestures of friendly smiles of courtesy. I approached him, and he said that he wanted to apologize and say thank you because he and his wife had just recently had a baby.

Let us choose our Father's words and not allow our natural flesh out of tradition control us. Remember, before it is a thought, it comes from a direction of life or death. Think about it.

Josiah the original Uncle Tom whose key was used by Harriet Beecher Stowe did not die during any of his beatings. He did finally escape, and his final residence was in Canada. He even met Queen Elizabeth, who looked at him and his woodcrafts and said, "So you are one of those fugitive slaves from America."

What Uncle Tom's Cabin did was cause a people group to start recognizing how we were devaluing lives that were created by God. We were making judgments on their lives in a moment of anger or sometimes just because, sometimes out of fear of what was assumed would happen.

Historically being referred to as an Uncle Tom has been viewed as a negative, but it should be the exact opposite. Standing up boldly for what you believe in to the point where you are beaten to death is not something to be ashamed of but to be revered. Think about it—if only we had more Uncle Toms.

After reading the following paragraph, which comes directly from the book *Uncle Tom's Cabin*, take a selah moment and think about it for yourself. I am proud to say I am an Uncle Tom. I continue to express my forgiveness to those who choose to continue to devalue life that came from the Creator Himself with purpose.

> Tom looked up to his master, and answered, "Mas'r, if you was sick, or in trouble, or dying, and I could save ye, I'd give ye my heart's blood; and if taking every drop of blood in this poor old body would save your precious soul Mas'r I'd give 'em freely, as the Lord gave his for me. O, Mas'r! don't bring this great sin on your soul! It will hurt you more than twill me! Do the worst you can, my troubles'll be over soon; but, if ye don't repent(change your mind), yours won't never end!"

Who is our final judge? Do we truly trust in His Word and what and how He feels concerning His creation in His own image? Before man acknowledged Jesus as the Messiah, He was known as Joseph's boy from Nazareth, the carpenter's son.

Eventually the passion-driven words in *Uncle Tom's Cabin* made it to President Lincoln's hands while he was facing these issues close to his heart. He was moved in such a way that he invited her to the White House, and it is said that he said to Harriet, "So you are the little lady who started this war."

Harriet Beecher Stowe was mercilessly taunted in various ways of mental abuse because not only was she a woman, but the words that were being written were hitting the core of the hearts of men and women whose thoughts were truly being led by the economy.

She received in the mail body parts of existing slaves with threats concerning her life and her family's safety. There is a quote from Harriett that has caused me to continue that says, "Never give up, for that is just the place and time that the tide will turn." We must cross the border of the slave plantation into the land of freedom!

She was exposing not only the character of Tom but many slaves' accounts, including slave traders, plantation slave owners, and Quakers, to name a few.

Chapter 16

# Slavery by Another Name

A s I *have chronicled these* events in history, it has been documented that consequently there was anger in the South because their economy went through a major overhaul. A lot of hearts were being touched by the governing of a truth, which was that we were all created equally by God with a purpose.

As we found ourselves entering the early 1870s, there were laws instated in various states—ridiculous laws, like no spitting in public. Some of these laws are still on the books but they are no longer used with any purpose today as they did back then. Remember, African Americans still were not as literate as the lighter-pigmented people groups in this country. (How did you like that approach in my change of thinking on the spot!)

These laws were used against the African American people group with a grave impression on the free African American population to a different enslavement. It was the chain gang. In this unjust atmosphere, we found ourselves once again determining the degrees of life accordingly.

When the thirteenth amendment was written in the Constitution on December 18, 1865, which officially outlawed slavery and involuntary servitude, for approximately twenty years there was a lull of oppression among the people groups until there was an idea of justification of looking at different people groups as being in different brackets of life. That justification came out of science in a book called *The Origin of Species* by Charles Darwin.

His personal experiences of his daughter, Annie, and a son who both died at an early age caused a passion and a thought process of eliminating a Creator while looking at a truth, better known as his theory of "the survival of the fittest." *The Origin of Species* caused a validation theory since his own personal circumstances were not acceptable. It was a classification of origins.

When I think about it, we all find ourselves in diverse situations that cause us to think, *How could a loving God allow these things to happen?* Actually, He did not allow them to happen. After the first Adam was created, God caused a change in the land with the authorities that had been given unto Adam, and God does not go back on His word. Adam was told not to eat of the tree because it would bring on death, and it did. But our Father had a backup plan for all of us—Jesus—and He kicked death in the teeth and rose up from the grave for whosoever believes.

At this same period of time, there was a eureka moment occurring over in England. The *Gilgamesh* epic was bringing forth evidence to a deluge or should I say a genocidal flood that was known by a people group in 2500 BC.

The *Gilgamesh* epic is the oldest form of writing on tablet that is known today, but it also in several ways parallels the Bible. For example, there is first the Flood and then there is a reference to a god creating man from the dust of the earth. There is also mention of a tree of immortality (i.e., the tree of life).

The curator's name who was unfolding these items in 1870 was George Smith. During his lengthy studies on the *Gilgamesh* epic, he came across the specific name of a man by the name of Noah. He became somewhat delirious as it is recounted as a time of him stripping himself of his external clothing while stating over and over again, "It is true! Those ancient Hebrew stories in the Bible are true!"

It hit the press in America at the same time that the announcement of *The Origin of Species* hit. It went from front page news to an article hidden among the others as general news.

Out of my studies, what I have found to be a constant pattern is that I am looking for details that line up with the Word of God, it will be hidden beneath the mundane, everyday news and will be looked upon as not worthy of reporting. As I step back with this fragment in my hand, I see a mosaic design of history with pieces missing that complete the whole, and as it all comes together, it is so beautiful.

As fragmented or hidden as the facts may be, we do have a Creator who loves us all, and He knows our priestly names if we want to claim them.

Chapter 17

# *What Defines Us*

A *maris was in a play* here in Virginia that was called *The Legend of Pocahontas.* During this play, several times over the audience found themselves coming out of the auditorium saying, "That was just wonderful. I did not know those things about Pocahontas and what happened right here in our own backyard." There were many tears and wondering minds. After seeing the play, I had another night of not being able to sleep, which I know many of you have had also. What I have found that helps me is to write them down, and now I have the pleasure of sharing my thoughts with you!

As I sat in my closet, these are some of the words that came to mind. The butterfly effect theory is a theory that a particular individual brought to other scientists' attention in 1963 that the motion of one butterfly's wings can affect the weather on the other side of the world. I approached the children with great excitement, which they are all so used to. They received it with the normal homeschool attitude of, "Thanks so much, Mom, for continuing to teach me even in my thirties." Well maybe not so much, but that is how I saw it. Thanks, kids!

As time continued, I heard a song by Deniece Williams called "Black Butterfly." Within the lyrics I heard the words,

"And let all of them who read it, remember when they need it, when their dreams are built on truth it will never die, butterfly."

I immediately said, "Guys, come to the kitchen." I expressed to them the butterfly effect theory based on the truth of the Word of God and this song. Then I played it, and there was another one of those "Aha!" moments of thought that occurs in our house quite regularly.

In the play, there is a scene where Pocahontas and John Smith and John Rolf are in London, and they sing a very harmonious song called, "If I Never Met You," which is sung preceding the scene of Pocahontas' death. I started to think this coincides with the butterfly effect. Out of the right thoughts, Pocahontas stood up in her culture. The right thoughts of John Smith led Pocahontas into a new language and new relationship with John Rolf, which in turn gave a new birth of oneness between two people groups being governed by one standard rule of truth—the Word of God! Only His Word can and continues to bring us together as one. He is the one who directs us by love, for God is love.

It was the goo-to-you perspective. Out of a superiority complex, we here in America started to see ourselves as different races according to Charles Darwin's studies. The African American people groups were pulling themselves out of one thought process of having no real purpose into a stance of life with value. Now they foresaw a future in America being walked out now as a division of people groups according to the monkey group.

Let us let truth define us.

Chapter 18

# The Curse of Ham

A *thought process begins to brew.* It is the superior and the inferior mindset. In the early 1900s, authors such as Carter G. Woodson believed that if you could convince an African American that his black face was a curse and that his struggle to change was hopeless, it would be the worst sort of lynching that could occur.

That same mindset rolled over into the churches as well. If we no longer look at ourselves from the six-day creation out of the Word that was spoken in the beginning by God, we find ourselves in the wilderness mentality. Adam and Eve's perspectives were skewed because they believed they did not have it all as far as having full knowledge of their status in the garden. They were persuaded to take and eat (senses) and they would become like God.

A little note of thought: they were already like God. They chose not to think on Gods words but on the sensual desires that were being tapped into. Take in the cursed perspective and watch what it churns out.

First comes guilt and shame. I don't think that was what they were going for exactly. There is killing, stealing, and of course destruction, especially in the mind. We in this generation believe from the Ham (darker people group) coming from a monkey group in the deeper parts of Africa. That is where it all starts to go really wrong.

Read your Bible. It does not say Ham was cursed; it was Canaan, his son, whose behavior of disrespect of his father is acknowledged. That is the curse on the descendants of Canaan. Ham did have other sons.

Children, honor your parents, for this is right as unto the Lord. This holds true for all of us. Let's cancel the wrong thoughts out with understanding. The Word of God says, "With all thy getting, get understanding." Let us call on Him for the wisdom in His Word, not the contrary, which will always contradict and say in your mind, "Did He really say that?" I truly believe that as is stated in Jeremiah 33:3, "Call on Him and He will hear you and He will show you great and mighty things that you know not of." As seen in the prodigal son's situation, he returned home from one mind-set of thinking, which was a "give me" state of mind. He returned home with a changed state of mind out of the love recognition of his father who was waiting for him to come home.

As an African American woman, I come back to my Father's house and say, "Dad, thank you for the woman you created me to be." And please don't hold on to those untruths that have seeped in, such as the curse of Ham.

Chapter 19

# The Hidden Perspective

I *am a homeschool mom, and* I would have frustrations when teaching my children Bible stories. Then in my mind I would think, *That was refreshing; now to the real world of teaching.* That was the wrong perspective, but it was the one I was more acquainted with after spending so many years under the tutelage of millions of years. It had a flow. I found myself dropping books, especially when my son asked me, "Mommy, where are the Africans?" during our Bible study and devotion time. I struggled because my mindset was, "Cursed in the jungles of Africa with bones in their noses and grass skirts, diseases and death which had and has been displayed in countless magazines and books."

The long of the short of all this is I really did not believe. I did not want to go there because my fear was great. I really struggled with my beliefs in the Word of God really being true. I struggled with millions of years of death and destruction. I became my parents, sitting at the kitchen table.

How I answered my son's question was with much study. It took a lot of digging to get past all the coverups of shame and justifications for bitterness to gather truths, especially coming from personal accounts that were not being written to cross paths with others but to tell their individual story.

Let's go back to the Garden of Eden perspective, willingly allowing God to magnify His name. Let His kingdom come and His will be done on earth as it is in heaven. Let truth go before our story. It is true. All things hidden shall be known. It all takes time and much studying.

Chapter 20

# Your Name Is Important

A*re we important enough for* our names to be remembered? Maybe we need to physically and emotionally act out of our pains of what we feel is unjust in our communities of thinking. I believe we are being duped into a way of thinking because we continue to look at our fellow man as the enemy. It takes our eyes off of the one who truly hates us—Satan, the father of all lies. He uses people with no recognition of the individual. His mission is to kill, steal, and destroy. It's on his written resume; look it up. Riddle me this—are we being duped? I really want to know.

I believe in taking notes from Jesus. Before Jesus went into the wilderness for the forty days, the last words for Him to remember were, "This is My beloved Son, in whom I am well pleased." It was heard by many but mainly by Jesus.

While in the wilderness, He was approached by the enemy with multiple accusations of, "If you be the son of God, then do this or that." He continued to retort with, "It is written."

Let us not forget that one thing the enemy did not understand was that He was not only the Son of God but the beloved Son. Keep in mind our identity in the eyes of God. When questions arise in our minds of who we are really, say to yourself, "I am the beloved son or daughter of the Most High God." It is written. Think about it.

In the Word, it is stated that before you were in your mother's womb, you were in the hands of God, and He knew your name. There is one who knows your name, and there is one who believes you are not important enough to remember your name. Are we living out a heavenly perspective of ourselves or to the contrary, as in the beginning, after sin and death entered this world through Adam's choice to disobey?

I choose to believe in the one who created me as an individual being coded (DNA) and fingerprinted by God. One of the most gripping aspects of slavery, demonically driven, was the fact that they did not want the slaves to know their names. Isaiah 49:1 says, "Listen to me, all of you in far-off lands! The Lord called me before my birth; from within the womb he called me by name."

**God Knows Me**

There are two females mentioned in the Bible, and their names are not mentioned, but their lives and actions to the living word of God are greatly acknowledged. They are the woman with the issue of blood and Jairus's daughter. Their positions in life are being acknowledged, so let's take the time to think about these two individuals who were known by God before they were even in their mother's wombs.

Stop, take a deep breath, and think about what came next. This was a woman who had been bleeding for twelve years. No one had been able to solve her issue. She was obviously carrying a continual stench, which caused her friends and family to stay away from her. It was a huge distraction in her life. Get the picture. There was a feeling of, "I have had enough of this," swelling up inside of her as she found out about Jesus coming into the town.

The twelve-year-old daughter of a man by the name of Jairus had reportedly died, and Jesus was on His way to this man's house, with reports of death ringing in the air. As Jesus was going through the town, the unnamed woman positioned herself to get through the crowd to just touch the hem of His religious shawl. That was all she wanted. It was strange for her to even think that stepping out like this and just touching the garment this individual was wearing would help her after twelve years of many practicing physicians diagnosis of no cure. In her mind, she felt it was right thinking. Why?

In the Jewish people group in their oral traditions, they had the handed down scrolls of accounts from the Old Testament, which was still yet a holding on mentality. There was a traditional waiting for the Messiah to come mentality. Obviously, in her situation she was stepping out in a belief that was narrow. The crowd that surrounded Jesus was the observation crowd, the cheering crowd, the religious crowd.

There she stood with a radical move of not wanting to be seen but wanting a change in her life. She had to step out of her comfort zone of solitude and make her way through the crowd, and what happened when she touched the garment! Jesus stopped, turned around, looked at her, and spoke to her, saying, "Take courage, daughter! Your faith has made you well" (Matt. 9:20–21). Her faith was acknowledged in the words of God that were handed down. Jesus spun around! Then He spoke to her courage, acknowledging her as daughter. Not only did she get acknowledged as daughter, but she was immediately healed of her total situation. Wow! I like that. How about you?

Then Jesus made His way to Jairus's house. His daughter was surrounded by the traditional mourners. Jesus sent them out, which was pretty radical, and they began to mock Jesus' words. He shut the door and spoke to what needed His attention, which seemed to be the dead, lifeless body of a child.

The words He spoke to her were, "Talitha cumi," which was interpreted to mean, "Damsel, arise." They thought she was dead, and there came Jesus saying, "Stop your traditional songs of mourning and get out!" She was considered dead in the natural eyes of man. In the eyes of Jesus, she was only sleeping.

We the older generation should question and study the steps we take while following the traditional crowds. We should step out and by faith reach out and touch the true and living God. By doing this, we are preparing the way for future generations to respond to the Word of God, which can and will bring life to any dead situation, but we have to step out and truly believe, for it is stated in the Word of God that your traditions have made the Word of God of no effect.

# Chapter 21

# *Traditions*

Traditionally speaking, when I found out I was carrying a new life in me at the time of crisis in my life, it would have been only right to terminate the pregnancy. With our fourth child being born at twenty-three weeks and feeling a bit overwhelmed emotionally, it would only be right.

Think about it—after finding out about my son's conception, traditionally there would have been a decision to make on life or death depending on the circumstance. The decision had already been made, and we actually had confidence in the hand that created that life and knowing what our situation entailed. What came out of this life was a freedom of the mind and a trust in His Word, which continues to increase day by day.

Out of His traditions of promises, I have attained life. I started out being blessed under grace without acknowledging it, and then I claimed it as my own actions causing the blessings. My famous quote was, "Three is enough for me." I found out that His blessings are above and beyond whatever we could think or imagine. Instead of three, God has blessed us with seven beautiful blessings, and their names in order are Patrice, Chiara, Little Morris (not so little now), Miracle Mary Elizabeth, James, Michael, and Amaris, and that's the whole enchilada, or should I say completion.

There is a tale that is told about a woman whose husband had gone out and gotten her the biggest ham to fix for their dinner. Out of his excitement, he watched as she prepared it, and to his dismay, she took out a big butcher knife, cut off a large portion of the ham, and threw it in the trash. The husband then inquired why she did that, and she said, "It has been a tradition in my family for years, starting with my great-grandmother." He then set out to respectfully find out why this tradition started, so he could justify in his mind why his wife had decided to throw this ham away! He then called her grandmother and asked her. Her explanation was that the pan was not large enough to hold such a large piece of ham. Let us not be led by mere traditions; they can take us away from the Promised Land.

Chapter 22

# *The Trial that Changed Minds*

I*n 1925 there was a* trial called the Scopes Trial, maybe better known as the Monkey Trial, which ended with a couple of things that caused great shifts in our public schools. There was a question-and-answer scene that caused a historical shift in our thinking here in America. The session went like this, as documented from the court's files. It was asked of a well-known statesman at the time by the name of William Jennings Bryan. He was standing in defense of the Bible as dictating the beginning as opposed to Darwin's theory. This question-and-answer session caused this entire shift, especially in our schools and in our legal system. The questions asked by Clarence Darrow were, in his own words, "To bring Bryan down."

From the reporter's memo:

Q: "Do you think the earth was created in six days?"
A: "Not six days of twenty-four hours ... My impression is they were periods ..."

Q: "Now if you call those periods, they may have been a very long time?"
A: "They might have been."

Q: "The creation might have been going on for a very long time?"

A: "It might have continued for millions of years."

At this point in time, it was like the church was on trial for its beliefs. Was the Word of God valid? According to Darrow and Bryan, maybe we can start cutting and pasting when it comes to the Word of God.

If we don't believe His Word from the beginning, we may as well join hands and agree.

I think that its interesting how these two individuals hold some of the same views as Charles Darwin and Sir Isaac Newton who are both buried side by side under the West Minster Abbey.

One was buried with a thought released based on theory the other released thoughts based on laws that just are and have not changed.

One countered the thoughts of a creator while the other believed in a creator.

Personally I like standing on something that is solid and does not change like the law of gravity we can dispute it but when we test it by jumping off a nearby building we come out with the same results. Just a thought!

Chapter 23

# *What Is Good?*

A*t this point, we as* a people group of a humankind once again start to look at each other as animals in an order that says some deserve to live and others don't. It's like road kill. For some animals, such as the cute puppies, we will swerve to keep from hitting them. Others, like a skunk, we may flinch before hitting them, but it's no big deal (survival of the cutest).

My question is in connection with these facts known to me as truths. In the beginning, as it was written in the Word of God, *yom* was a Hebrew term used to signify a twenty-four-hour day. Also in the beginning, after God had spoken everything into being, He said it was all good. There was no death or diseases in the land.

How do we explain the millions of years of death and disease as we cut and paste in this realm of thinking? Is that good? I don't think that is good. That is my own interpretation. This is where I draw the line (which came from the Bible). I believe every word from the Bible, from Genesis to Revelation, to be true, and I will continue to stand on my beliefs.

Just think about this scenario from the Bible. Jesus' first miracle was at a wedding. In this time, it was customary to start a banquet with the best wine. They ran out of wine, and Mary said, "Go ask Jesus. He will know what to do." Jesus in the fleshy mind-set wondered if He was in position. At this point I see Jesus saying, "Let's take it to the beginning and tell it like it is." He instructed some gentlemen to take not two or three cisterns but specifically six cisterns and fill them to the brim.

Now let's talk about these cisterns that sat outside the synagogue. They were used as cleansing vessels for the sacrifices, so I don't believe this was fresh spring water. He did not tell them to empty them and then fill them. He just said fill them to the brim. (Get the picture—nasty, right!) That's not all, folks; He then told them to take a cup of it to the master of the ceremony. Now what was the master of the ceremonies looking for? You are right, good wine! Not so much—at least not in our own eyes.

There is another point here: if he is given anything but what he asked for, due to customs, that put the servants in the position to be killed. It remained in its watery state until he took it and drank it. At this point, I can feel the servant's hearts racing and his thoughts of blame pointing toward Jesus. However, not only was this wine; it was great wine. Whew!

The master of ceremonies commented on it being the best wine and also asked, "Why are we serving this last?" My mind had problems with this situation because I just looked at this part of the Bible and took it to say that it is okay to drink wine, right! Well not so much for me because I ended up in various unwanted positions in my life because of my own justifications with these Scriptures. I was enlightened one day to see this in a way that made me say, "Wow, that makes sense and once again connects me in right relation with a loving God."

Okay! Six cisterns, dirty water, words spoken by Jesus, obedience taking place, six cisterns immediately transformed, not only into wine but the best wine of the evening. My eyes were opened to a new way of understanding. Basically it boils down to this: Jesus can speak and His words can instantly change a natural substance. In my knowledge, which is not that vast in the wine-making business, I believe it takes several years for there to be a good wine made out of grapes.

When Jesus spoke the words, they were respected and obeyed. Let us think for a minute. As we continue in our lives, there are many moments when we feel like our lives stink like the stinky water.

Jesus says, "Keep walking out what I promised."

Remember, Noah continued to build the ark with no water. Remember Abraham with Isaac: "Kill the only-begotten son that was promised out of Sarah's womb." That situation stunk, but he continued to walk it out. Joseph was sold into slavery, but he continued. Remember Moses with his guilt and speech impediment, and the Word of "I Am" continued. With Shadrach, Meeshach, and Abednego, it was hot, but they continued get the picture. Esther said, "If I perish, I perish." She continued. Mary said, "So be it unto me," and continued. Let us continue to walk out the stinky sacrificial waters to the Master of the ceremonies as He tastes and sees that it is the best He created us to be. The final note is this: "Well done my good and faithful servant." Now that is the very best! Think about it.

God said, "And it was, in six days and He called it good." All six cisterns changed immediately through the Last Adam's words, which had authority on this earth to change a sin nature back to the way it was in the beginning in to God's nature, which is the best. If it were not true, the skeptics would have definitely stopped the press on this one concerning the six cisterns.

The same has occurred in my life and my mind-set. I can testify to that personally, and with that I say thank You, Lord, for thinking about us from the beginning. As I continue to walk with the stinky sacrificial waters of my daily life, I keep my eyes on the words Jesus sent me out with, continuing to trust in His words and leaning not on my own understanding. With my understanding, I start to look around at the glasses on the table that have actual wine in them. Actually, that is the best wine because it was served first. They are having a good time while here I am continuing to walk out some dirty water. This is a narrow way of going about things. Okay, I reach the Master, and He says this is the best and looks at me. I am now in the image of God as in the beginning. All of these things are mine. I possess all good in me. As I continue to walk out the naturalness of this mind-set here on earth, continuing to renew it according to His Word, it continues to come out not only good but the best.

Others look and see that the Lord God is good and His mercies endure forever and ever. He is no respecter of persons, only a respecter of faith. As it is written in Psalm 14:1, "For a fool says in his heart that there is no God." My mom did not raise a fool! And I hope the same is true for you. Think about it (Jer. 33:11 AMP).

It is quite all right for you to call me crazy. Just remember that only crazy people can see what I can see. The truth is prevailing and shall prevail whatever we may think about it. I just came to tell you that the truth will be this world's insanity. God is not a special guest to our group sessions or discussions. The truth is that we all have fallen short in our natural man mind-set. As we so choose to believe, there are no exemptions in this system, which is called the kingdom of God's system. I believe that we are all called with special orders set in us as we choose to see ourselves out of the eyes of the one who created us. The inspiration for my initial thought came out of a song I listen to quite often called "The Truth Is" by Lisa McClendon. It is a great song! Truth always overrides scrutiny.

## We All Fall Short

Speaking of us all falling, I was flipping through channels on a Sunday morning and found it very disturbing that out of 899+ channels on this television, there were only ten channels making reference to the acknowledgment of God.

So where are we with our thinking? After seeing that, I felt that our attention is being drawn away by false teachers. Lots of sensual desires of the eye are being drawn in to satisfy a feeling, sometimes good and sometimes bad according to the flesh.

Simultaneously I found myself watching a report on a football game at Penn State that Joe Paterno did not attend because of a questionable situation with one of his assistant coaches. It first came to his attention when the coach was seen in a shower with a young man. It was reported to the coach, and long story short, the accused coach was not taken off the team. It's been approximately ten to fifteen years that this has continued with different individuals. Joe Paterno, who was the coach at Penn State for some forty-six years, was being fired from his coaching position for his failure to deal with the situation. As I listened to a large portion of the media's way of portraying the whole situation, it was the sadness of the loss that tugged at my heart, even the flowers being placed at Paterno's front door. People were saying prayers outside his house. It started making me feel more compassion toward Paterno.

After all of this, they showed a woman at a table outside the stadium in blue, pen in hand, representing the supporters of the victims—the children. At this point, my feelings were, "How could she be doing that with all these mourners for Joe Pa with his absence at the game?"

Whose support should we uphold, God's or man's? There is a right and wrong to this situation, and looking at the fallout, it made me sad at how we can so easily be misled by mere feelings.

Our attention is being drawn in such a way that it is sort of scary. Unaware, we are being drawn by our senses to be more compassionate to a wrong than to a right. Just look at all of the channels and all of the shows. Are they leading to acknowledge the Father of truth or the father of all lies? One came to give us life more abundantly, and the other came to kill, steal, and destroy. It is up to us to open our eyes, expose the originator to all these situations that are being brought before our eyes, and take captive our thoughts. And we must stop being led by our fleshly desires, which will lead us to hell. These are not my words. That is what Dad told me; either we believe Him or we don't.

Chapter 24

# Choose to Think about Your Thoughts

Come on! *If we don't* stand up and use what God has given us between the portholes of what we hear and what we see, we are continuing this vicious cycle of life and death. In the beginning, Adam and Eve heard words from the one creature other than themselves who was allowed a voice by a gracious God to still repent but denied it to what ruled him, which was desire. This desire he used as a temptation to the ones who had authority on this earth (human beings). His words were and still are, "Did He really say that? Eat this and you can become like God."

Remember at this point he had the make-up of an animal. At that point humans still carried authority, but now they were subject to death. Their relationship with God was severed. They took on sin and hid themselves, but God committed the first death of a life without sin as a symbol of covering with blood. At this point they felt they could converse with God.

Sacrifices were carried out after that, and God took a dead womb (Sarah's) and brought forth life. Abraham displayed his obedience with his only-begotten son from God. He referred to it as worship when he was taking his son to be sacrificed. God then provided him with a ram in the bush.

A people group came out of the lineage of Abraham's son, Isaac. Jacob continued to believe in this God that his son Joseph believed in, which brought them into the land of Egypt. This land, after four hundred years, turned from favored ground into enslavement. The hand of God saved the sons of the lineage of the believers through Moses. God led them through an individual who had a speech impediment. He kept them from several plagues the final death by recognizing the covering of blood of an innocent lamb over their doorposts. The Israelites were brought out of bondage, as was prophesied four hundred years prior to Joseph, who requested for his bones to be buried in the Promised Land. If it were not acknowledged as a truth from God, I don't believe they would have remembered the bones part.

In the beginning, God said to Satan, "I will put enmity between you and the woman's seed." God created in women a barrier in their wombs where the mother's blood does not mix with her child's. That was set up for us. Mary's blood of sin nature never mixed with Jesus' blood (perfect without blemish). Throughout their oral traditions, the Israelites continued to tell of the God who saved them and would send the Messiah. When Mary said, "So be it unto me," she received out of what she believed by faith through the words of the angel Gabriel sent by God. She then received the nature of God, who was sinless, into her. I believe she was the first to receive salvation as she came to the cross and then as He entered the room after His resurrection.

John 3:16 says, "For God so loved the world that He gave His only begotten Son that whosoever believes in Him [so be it unto me!] shall not parish but have everlasting life."

Thoughts become words. (Oh what thoughts God has toward us if we want to believe.)

Words then become action. (There's a King inside of me. He's the man that you cannot see.)

Actions become character. (My life is a brochure of the kingdom of God.)

Character is everything!

## There Are No Qwinkie Dinks

Things to think about: In 1947 a powerful microscope was invented, and through the lens there was a wonderful discovery. We were no longer looking at a cell and identifying it as goo. There were things inside it that now needed to be identified.

In 1947, the Dead Sea Scrolls were discovered! "Skeptical minds of the Bible are being addressed in many ways." Writings from 250 BC were matching up with the King James Version of the Bible written in 1611. Two scrolls were found totally intact—the Isaiah scroll and the Genesis scroll. In Genesis 3:5 God said "through His seed"—not seeds but seed. Chapter 62 of the Isaiah scroll read by Jesus, and He proclaimed, "I am the one." He then walked out that prophecy.

## Where's the Standard

In 1975, doctors and scientists came together off the coast of California to state, "Houston, we have a problem. It's called DNA!" DNA is a specific code given to each individual of its kind (human being) with an order. Who is the designer? Dr. Behe was one who came out of this meeting with a thought perspective that we hear today as the intelligent design movement. This is what caused the waters of thought in science to shift ever so slightly. Scientists said, "Let's just call it intelligent design."

In 1992, the Hubble telescope identified a galaxy by the name of "the X structure," which is the core of the whirlpool galaxy. Resembles the cross with Christ. It makes you think. We are steadily looking for life outside of God, and as intelligent as we think we are, our loving God continues to remind us of who He is, from the tiniest form of life under the microscope to as far out in space as we can go. Still we find that there is a special quality in this earth's life that is set in an order of safety by the one who created all order and laws, such as gravity. God is the Alpha and the Omega, the beginning and the end.

You choose—is it man's words or God's words that will be the standard of what is the truth? Truth prevails and continues to stand unchanged. Think about it!

I just finished the 10k of Richmond, Virginia! I saw something so interesting that made me think. There were very large posters from a school project in Richmond that stated, "What I stand for." One said they stood for their self-portrait as an African American. Another stood for their love of dogs and nature, vampires, colors, random things, and last but not least, my paintings. As I was walk-jogging, I started to think. It is really sad to think that a part of our future generation has no real solid thought perspective as to what they stand for because obviously there is so much change that we can't rely on anything to stand on. Where's the standard?

**I Leave You with Peace**

As you can tell, I love getting out and walking or running when I am in condition. The one thing I enjoy most, especially since I started doing the 10k in Richmond, is when I reach the halfway mark. Many can testify to this with me that this is a sight that is just breathtaking. As you make that turn and your metabolism begins to rise with the energy that surrounds you with the crowd, you look up and it is a sight like no other. There is a sea of people all running in the same direction. When I see this, it encourages me not only to finish the race but to continue in this race to see many going to Heaven in excitement as we run together with the same hope in Christ Jesus, believing that whosoever will shall be saved.

Believing that God is our Creator and that we truly are related brings us into a thought pattern called love. You know God is love. Jesus said when asked what the greatest commandment is, "This is the greatest commandment, first love the Lord your God with all your heart, mind, and all of your strength. And love your neighbor as I have loved you" Well I believe the Pharisees thought they would trick Him, but we are talking about Jesus and if you look carefully, what you see here are those words *heart, mind,* and *strength.* Now I have a question: if you love someone, will you kill him? What about stealing from him? You get the picture. Now go down the list of Ten Commandments and tell me which one you would do intentionally if you really loved somebody. Jesus wants us to look at Him, and then He asks us, "Do you love Me?" Think about it.

I can see the love that was demonstrated to us on the cross with Jesus taking all of my sins on the cross so I could clothe myself in His righteousness. Let me explain it this way: Jesus made no work efforts of sin. He was taking on this position, and yes, He allowed this process because of that word we use so frequently without recognizing the real truth to it all: love. He died a death that we were set up to take through the first Adam out of the first sin. We are the natural descendants genetically speaking. The Last Adam sent by God through His blood, our redeemable bloodline. We can recognize this when our standard of belief is that His Word is truth.

Jesus Christ was the promised seed of God sent to save the world, not to condemn the world. All prophecies had come to pass through Christ Jesus. It is our responsibility to recognize and take all our thoughts outside of His Word captive to the Word of God and watch. All things do work together for good as long as our eyes are set on right perspective.

While teaching a class called "Demolishing Strongholds" out of my home, we were truly blessed, and I wanted to share with you as I come to a close. Please take these words to heart and let God's Word continue to lead you in life everlasting. Second Timothy 4:3–7 says, "For the time is coming when (people) will not tolerate (endure) sound and wholesome instruction, but, having ears itching (for something pleasing and gratifying), they will gather to themselves one teacher after another to a considerable number, chosen to satisfy their own liking and to foster the errors they hold. And will turn aside from hearing the truth and wander off into myths and man-made fictions."

May grace and peace be multiplied unto you with the understanding of our Lord and Savior Jesus Christ. Amen.

Chapter 25

# *What about the Children and the Generations to Come?*

### Chiara's Story
### 1992

A*lot of people know us* as that big family with the parents that, shockingly enough, are the parents of all the children. But before that time, there was just us—me and my big sister Patrice. Three years after my birth came the first son, Morris II. When Morris came, I can recall holding him on the couch. With his big cheeks and squinty eyes, he was the little king. But we three didn't know, didn't expect, and still can't fully explain 1992.

That's the year Mary was born.

I don't recall the Sunday-morning church service or Bible study that inspired my mom to get her tubes untied. I remember her coming home after the surgery. I remember my dad holding her arm and helping her out of the car. I remember thinking, *Man, having babies really hurts,* not knowing she wasn't pregnant yet.

I don't even remember her telling us she was pregnant, but I do remember the day Morris fell off the swing. I remember my mom, then pregnant, running across the field carrying him toward us at the park. I didn't know it then, but this was the day I was getting ready to have a little sister.

I don't remember my mom being rushed to the hospital, but I do remember the call that came the day before my dad's birthday, three days before my birthday: "Chiara you have a little sister." Then I remember the day of our first visit. The small sink where you washed your hands with little sponges filled with soft prickly spikes on one side. The long, dark hallway flanked by windows. The robes having to be tied and rolled up that were obviously too large for small children. The hair nets, the masks. Walking into the room where Mary was, expecting big cheeks and squinting eyes. Finding what looked like a baby bird on an operating table covered with a thin sheet of plastic over her lit up little box of a bed. That was my sister. As I stood among the beeping machines, in the dimly lit room, I remember thinking, *This is normal*, not knowing this was a miracle.

Each time they moved Meme, as we called her, she became the new sickest baby in the room. We drew her pictures so she could think of us when we weren't there. Babies died in those rooms—helpless little babies. That's when thoughts churned. Why the babies? This can't be fair! Poor and rich babies, death didn't care. Abandoned babies and loved babies, it didn't matter. I never thought Mary would die, but the doctors did, and once I remember she did die.

As a child, I pictured that moment as one of panic. As sounds filled the air in the room with beeps and screeching, doctors and nurses were falling over each other for what little room her tiny incubator allowed. Somewhere between a doctor and nurse, a mother's eyes fell on her child. Then the unthinkable. My mom said, "Mary is in God's hands. He is caring for her." And she calmly walked away. Mary survived, and people were changed forever by that moment. How could someone have such faith? They were always baffled by my mom, but I knew they respected her ability to believe.

Understanding how fragile life is at an early age is a gift and a curse. My friends all couldn't wait to grow up. I loved being that age, whatever that age was. Around the third grade, I took one of Mary's breathing tubes in for show and tell. After other students got up to show off their favorite stuffed animal or video game, I got up with the tube. As the students passed the thin, long tube around the room, I told Mary's story. I told them about how the doctors said that she had a 1 percent chance of making it through her first day. Then I went on to tell the room, "We all have that same chance every day. You could die on your way home. Life can change in a moment." While I'm sure the teacher appreciated the inspiration and passion of my speech, she wasn't 100 percent on board with the whole "terrifying my fellow classmates into appreciating life" and had a few words with my parents about what was appropriate for show and tell.

Mary recently graduated from high school, and I keep her graduation picture at my desk as a constant reminder that God is real and miracles do happen. This story reached far beyond my family. Mary was in medical journals and dubbed the miracle baby. About a month ago, someone I knew as a child started working at my company, where I do benefits orientations. As part of the orientation, I normally tell people how expensive hospital rooms are, and that day I used Mary's story as an example but didn't use her name. The young woman stopped the orientation and said, "I remember Mary. Her story really touched my life." It's moments like that one when I'm reminded that God is working even when we don't see His hand.

*—Chiara*

Chapter 26

# Love of Eighty-Eight Keys

As a child, my family would go to Ohio to visit my relatives during the summer. One of my fondest memories of these trips was watching my grandfather play the piano. My grandfather had taught himself how to play years and years ago. But now in his old age, he found his audience with the children who visited his home in Cleveland. The old man would slowly sit down on the bench and begin playing fun and upbeat tunes. One song in particular I will never forget. While this jingle was simple, its harmonic melody stuck in the head of a developing six-year-old boy.

As time went by, my grandfather's health continued to deteriorate. Eventually my grandfather died. I was thirteen at the time and could not think of a personal experience I had with my grandfather. At the funeral, different relatives kept emotionally talking about their time they had with the man they called Strudwick. There were so many stories, from him working in the church to his days in the Navy, even tales of his childhood told by my ninety-eight-year-old Great Aunt Lily. My mother is her namesake.

I went home pondering a common interest that my grandfather and I shared. I continued to deliberate about what connection we had in the weeks following. In everything I would do, down to taking out the trash and doing schoolwork, I would wonder if it had any connection with my grandfather. I was beginning to wonder if I had anything in common with him other than my middle name.

About four months after my grandfather's funeral, I began studying and playing piano. I really enjoyed it and felt like I was decent at it. After many lessons, my teacher wanted to show me how to play a song. It was the harmonious tune from my childhood. As I played the song, I realized that my grandfather affected me in greater ways than I thought. By the time I had mastered the song, I realized that without my grandfather playing those songs when I was younger, I would have never had a love for the piano. No matter how many different songs I learn to play, I know it's all because of him. Every time I play piano, I remember my grandpa and how he had the same love and passion for this instrument with eighty-eight keys.

—James

CPSIA information can be obtained
at www.ICGtesting.com
Printed in the USA
BVHW03*1122200818

525056BV00007B/35/P